United States. Continental Army

General Orders Issued by Major-General Israel Putnam

United States. Continental Army

General Orders Issued by Major-General Israel Putnam

ISBN/EAN: 9783744784221

Printed in Europe, USA, Canada, Australia, Japan

Cover: Foto ©ninafisch / pixelio.de

More available books at **www.hansebooks.com**

GENERAL ORDERS

ISSUED BY

MAJOR-GENERAL ISRAEL PUTNAM,

WHEN IN COMMAND OF THE

HIGHLANDS,

IN THE SUMMER AND FALL OF

1777.

EDITED BY

WORTHINGTON CHAUNCEY FORD.

BROOKLYN, N. Y.:

HISTORICAL PRINTING CLUB.

1893.

hu . hu . hu .

INTRODUCTORY NOTE.

Early in May, Washington, governed by his anxiety for the safety of the Highlands, and harassed by the uncertainty of the enemy's movements, wished to place a Major-General in command on the Hudson. Arnold was first appointed; but he was too much engaged in seeking a "vindication" from a slight passed upon him by Congress in some recent promotions. Putnam was then selected. On May 24th, Washington wrote to the President of Congress: "I have sent General Putnam to command in that quarter;" but the choice was determined upon some time before. For McDougall, who was in command at Peekskill, was informed of it as early as the 16th, and the wish expressed that he would find his command "a happy one." General Parsons, then superintending the recruiting in Connecticut, was also ordered to Peekskill, to remain there until further orders.

Exactly when Putnam assumed command, I have been unable to determine; but it must have been about June 1st, and on that day he issued an order constituting a court martial. The interest of the campaign of 1777 centered on the incursion from Canada under Burgoyne, and the Highlands were the pivotal point. I sought long before I found a copy of the General Orders issued by Putnam during the summer and fall of 1777, but was finally rewarded by discover-

(1)

ing a mutilated record in the Connecticut Historical Society.

The entries began with that of July 19th, and in the regiment with which Sergeant Daniel Ware was connected, and ended when that regiment was ordered to join the main Continental army under Washington. After I had received a copy of Ware's book, further inquiries produced from the cabinet of the New York Historical Society a second record, kept by Major Richard Platt, of McDougall's brigade, more full and complete than the Connecticut Sergeant's, but still lacking some entries. Further interest is given to Platt's books by the fact that half of one volume is in McDougall's *MS.* This record also ceases in the fall, when Washington ordered the Brigade to join him in the Jerseys.

The following orders are, therefore, taken from two sources, and may be readily distinguished by the erratic spelling of Sergeant Ware. The entries to July 19th are taken from Platt; after that date Ware's record is taken as the basis, and where a word, name or phrase is inserted from Platt, it is printed in italics. Where the orders for a day, or a paragraph, is taken from Platt, it is not printed in italics, the spelling being sufficient to distinguish its authorship. I have inserted in [ ] the full names of the officers, where ascertainable; but the absence of any official roster of Massachusetts has made it impossible to be as complete as could be wished. Where Platt varies essentially from Ware, I have inserted the variation in ( ) and italics. The map is a copy, somewhat reduced in size, of one prepared by Claude Joseph Sauthier, in 1774, and published by William Faden.

In conclusion I wish to express my appreciation of the permissions granted me by the Historical Societies of Connecticut and New York, and of the courteous assistance given by the Secretaries, Mr. Frank B. Gay, of Hartford, and Mr. William Kelby, of New York. For the map I am indebted to Harvard University and its able librarian, Mr. Justin Winson. I am also indebted to Mr. Albert C. Bates, of Hartford, for his accurate and painstaking transcript of the Ware Orderly Book.

WORTHINGTON CHAUNCEY FORD.

Brooklyn, N. Y., October, 1892.

ORDERLY BOOK.

HEAD QUARTERS, PEEKSKILL, 1 JUNE, 1777.

Parole, *Mifflin*.   C. Sign, *Knox*.

The Court Martial of which Col? [Edward] Wigglesworth was President is dissolved.

L! Col? [Giles] Russel[1]
Brigade Major Marshall   } Field Officers for to-morrow.
Adjutant [   ] St. John

James Murphey a Private in Cap! Pearcy's* Comp? Col? [Henry B.] Livingston's Reg! tried at a Gen! Court Martial whereof Col? [Edward] Wigglesworth was President, for endeavoring to perswade Negroes to inlist in order to join Roger's Rangers†—For getting drunk & suspected of going to the Enemy, the Court found him guilty and sentence him to receive fifty Lashes on his bare Back.

William Mitchel ‡ of Col? [Philip Burr] Bradley's Reg! tried at the above Court Martial for Desertion, the Court found him guilty & sentence him to receive one hundred Lashes upon his bare Back.

Thomas Doyle ‖ of Col? Sam! [B.] Webb's Regiment tried at the above Court Martial for Desertion the Court found him guilty & sentence him to receive 39 Lashes on his bare back.

Micajah Foy of Cap! Goodall's [or Goodale] Company in Col? [Rufus] Putnam's Reg! tried at the same Court Martial for threatning to desert,—the Court sentence him to receive 39 Lashes on his bare back.

* Captain Jonathan Pearsee, of the 3d Company.

† The Queen's Rangers was a corps raised by Major Robert Rogers, of New Hampshire. This corps was famous during the contest, first under the command of Rogers, and after he went to England, under the lead of Simcoe.

‡ Of Sanford's Company.

‖ Of Middletown. He was in the Company of Captain John Hart.

(5)

Michael Poor a Private in Capt. Leavenworth's* Compy., Colo. [William] Douglass's Regt. was tried at the same Court Martial for getting drunk, endeavoring to force the guard & speaking treasonable language against the States of America, the Court found him guilty & sentence him to receive 100 Lashes on his Bare Back.

John Collins a private in Capt. Willington's Compy. in Colo. [Edward] Wigglesworth's Regt. tried at the same Court Martial for sleeping on his post, the Court find him guilty & sentence him to receive 50 Lashes.

Thomas Lane of Colo. [Israel] Angel's Regt. tried at the same Court Martial for selling his clothes, that were delivered him from the Continental Store, the Court found him guilty & sentence him to receive 100 Lashes & also orders that the Paymaster of the Regt. to which he belongs make stoppages of the one half of the Prisoner's Pay untill the Clothes he has sold be paid for.

The Genl. approves of the several sentences and orders the Corporal Punishment to be inflicted to-morrow morning at guard mounting.

After Orders.

The Officers of the different Guards to make their Reports to the Officer of the Day at Relieving Guards on the Grand parade.

HEAD QUARTERS, PEEKSKILL, 2 JUNE, 1777.

Colo. [Edward] Wigglesworth
Brigade Major [David] Smith } Field Officers for to-morrow.
Adjutant Tucker

HEAD QUARTERS, PEEKSKILL, 3 JUNE, 1777.

Parole, *Rariton.* C. Sign, *Somersett.*

Lt. Colo. [Peter] Regnier
Brigade Major Lord } Field Officers of the day.
Adjutant Wait

A detachment from Commdr. [Isaac] Sherman's Brigade consisting

* Eli Leavenworth, of New Haven. On 27 May, 1777, he was promoted from Captain to Major, but he had not learned this at the date of the order.

of 1 C 2 S 2 S 3 C 45 P to parade to-morrow morning at 6 o'clock at Gen! McDougalls Q˞s. A Detachment of the like Number to parade at the same time & place from Comm˯ᵈᵗˢ [Van] Cortlandt's & Livingston's Brigades. The Officers commanding them will apply to Head Quarters this Evening for Orders. Major Cranston's Effects to be sold to-morrow at 10 o'clock a. m., at Barracks No. 2.

--- ---

HEAD QUARTERS, PEEKSKILL, 4 JUNE, 1777.

Parole, *Wilmington.*   C. Sign, *Virginia.*

L! Col? Stacy

B. Major [Elihu] Marshall   } Field Officers for to-morrow.

Adj! Learned

There being Occasion for a Number of Men to go in whale Boats to cruize up & down the River—The Gen! orders that such as are acquainted with the Business do parade at H⁴ Q˞s to-morrow Morning.

The Gen! having observed that the Soldiers Quartered in Houses have abused them in a most scandalous Manner by pulling the Boards off, desires the officers will pay particular attention to it & let no man go unpunished.

--- ---

HEAD QUARTERS, [PEEKSKILL,] 5 JUNE, 1777.

Major [Benjamin] Ledyard

B. Major [David] Smith   } Officers for to-morrow.

Adjutant Frost

There being a large quantity of Flour & Wheat in Col? [Samuel] Drake's Mill, the Gen! directs that there be a Corp˞ˡˢ Guard mounted there till further orders and to receive their Orders from Col? Drake.

The Court of Enquiry whereof Col? [Philip Van] Cortlandt was President is dissolved. The Effects of Major Cranston to be sold to-morrow at 10 o'clock near Barracks No. 2.

HEAD QUARTERS, PEEKSKILL, 6 JUNE, 1777.

Major [Ebenezer] Grey
B. Major Lord   } Officers of the Day for to-morrow.
Adj.̈ Pearl

The Gen.̈ Court Martial whereof Brigadier Gen.̈ George Clinton was president is dissolved.

A number of Blacksmiths being immediately wanted, such as are good workmen will parade to-morrow at H.ᵈ Q.ʳˢ at 8 o'clock.

HEAD QUARTERS, PEEKSKILL, 7 JUNE, 1777.

Parole, *Nixon*.   C. Sign, *Varnum*.

There being a number of Wheelwrights wanted for the use of the army—

The Gen.̈ desires those who are acquainted with that Branch of Business will parade at Head Quarters to-morrow morning at Guard Mounting.

L.̈ Col.̈ [Matthew] Mead
B. Major [Elihu] Marshall   } Officers for to-morrow.
Adjutant Holden

HEAD QUARTERS, PEEKSKILL, 8 JUNE, 1777.

Parole, *Spencer*.   C. Sign, *Parsons*.

Lt. Col.̈ [Ebenezer] Sproul *
B. Major [David] Smith   } Officers for to-morrow.
Adjutant [Peter] Sacket

Henry B. Livingston arrested by order of Brigadier Gen.̈ Mc-Dougall for traducing the conduct of Brigadier Gen.̈ McDougall in ordering the Retreat of the Continental Troops on 23.ᵈ March last.

For neglecting to bring down his Regiment in Time on that Day, altho' ordered in time, 'till the Enemy was near the Town & then it was unprovided with Ammunition.

For ordering M.̈ Smith doing the Duty of Major of Brigade for his Brigade not to turn parties out of it unless the Orders were

* Force gives *Sprout*.

directed to him (the Colonel) which is contrary to the usage of the army by which he has embarrassed the Service.

For delaying the Returns of his Reg.̱ & Brigade by orders & whims of his own contrary to the known Rules of the Army & thereby delaying the Gen.̱ Returns of the Army in this Department.

For abusive Language to Gen.̱ McDougall at his own Quarters on 23.ᵈ Instant, unbecoming an Officer and a Gentleman in the presence of many Officers of the Army.

Col.̣ Henry B. Livingston being tried by the Gen.̱ Court Martial of which B. Gen.̱ George Clinton was President—

The Court after having duly considered the Proofs and Allegations of the parties specifyed in their Report, Returns & other papers offered in Evidence & the Written Defence of Col.̣ Livingston therewith delivered, are of Opinion, that tho' the Conduct of Brigadier Gen.̱ McDougall in ordering the Retreat of the Continental Troops on the 23.ᵈ March last stands unimpeach'd to this Court, yet no sufficient Evidence hath been offered to prove that Col.̣ Livingston hath traduced Gen.̱ McDougall's Conduct in that respect, & it appears to this Court that tho' Col.̣ Livingston's Reg.̱ was at that time unprovided with a sufficiency of ammunition, that it did not proceed from any criminal Neglect of his own. The Court do therefore adjudge & determine that the s.ᵈ Col.̣ Livingston is not guilty of the above two Charges. The Court is further of Opinion that the s.ᵈ Col.̣ Livingston is not guilty of ordering his Brigade Major not to turn parties out of it unless the Orders were directed to him the Col.̣ . But as to the Charge against the s.ᵈ Col.̣ Livingston of neglecting to bring down his Reg.̱ on 23.ᵈ March last & the delaying the Returns of his Reg.̱ & Brigade, by Orders & whims of his own, contrary to the known Rules of the Army, & thereby delaying the Gen.̱ Returns of the Army in this Department—The Court is [of] Opinion that the s.ᵈ Col.̣ Livingston is thereof guilty. The Court is further of Opinion as to the last Charge for abusive Language to Gen.̱ McDougall at his own Quarters on 23.ᵈ Instant unbecoming an Officer and Gentleman in the presence of many Officers of the Army, that tho' Col.̣ Livingston appears to this Court to be guilty of great Imprudence & Indiscretion in some parts of his Language & Conduct towards the Gen.̱.with respect to a Return made by the Col.̣ to the Gen.̱ yet his Conduct & Language was not such as will warrant the appellation of being unbecoming a Gentleman & Officer. The Court do therefore UNANIMOUSLY adjudge & determine, that considering the Nature of the Offence whereof they find Col? Henry B. Livingston guilty, and the Consequences thereupon attendant, that Col? Henry B. Livingston be reprimanded for his Offences in Gen! Orders for this Department and cautioned against the Commission of the like in future.*

The Gen! approves the judgment of the Court but nevertheless laments there should ever be a necessity of publickly reproving any Gentleman, particularly of so respectable Rank as Colonel. The consequences of the smallest Delay in the Execution of any order, are evidently most dangerous, & the least wilful neglect of this Nature too serious to be passed in Silence—equally ruinous and to be exploded is an indirect Compliance and every practical Equivocation.

In the Formation of an Army, rigorous Subordination cannot be too strictly adhered to. Breach of Respect to a Superior is an implicit Countenance to an Offence of a similar and more aggravated Nature with Inferiors & tends directly to the Subversion of Order.

The Gen! takes this opportunity to warn all Ranks against similar offences, hopes however this Caution is needless, & flatters himself he shall have no future Occasion to think it otherwise.

Col? Henry B. Livingston is released from his arrest & ordered to return to his Duty.

The Col?s & Comm? Officers of Corps must see that the Arms of their Reg?s & Detachments are immediately Branded, agreeable to a former order.

The Brand may be had at H? Q?s & must be carefully returned.

HEAD QUARTERS, PEEKSKILL, 9 JUNE, 1777.

Parole, *Montgomery.*   C. Sign, *Constitution.*

Major [Warham] Parks
Brigade Major Lord   } Officers for to-morrow.
Adjutant Smith

* The proceedings of this Court are printed in *Calendar of New York Historical Manuscripts*, II., 153.

HEAD QUARTERS, PEEKSKILL, 10 JUNE, 1777.

Parole, *Heath.*   C. Sign, *Independence.*

L! Col? [Frederick] Weissenfelts ⎫
B. Major [Elihu] Marshall   ⎬ Officers for to-morrow.
Adjutant St. John   ⎭

HEAD QUARTERS, PEEKSKILL, 11 JUNE, 1777.

Parole, *Franklin.*   C. Sign, *Conway.*

L! Col? [Calvin] Smith   ⎫
B. Major [David] Smith   ⎬ Officers for to-morrow.
Adjutant Obrian   ⎭

HEAD QUARTERS, PEEKSKILL, 12 JUNE, 1777.

Parole, *Green.*   C. Sign, *Providence.*

Major [Joseph?] Hart   ⎫
B. Major [Richard] Platt   ⎬ Officers for to-morrow.
Adjutant Glenny   ⎭

The Gen! is astonished to see everything that's bro't to Market
held up at such an unreasonable Rate. He acquaints the Gentleman Officers of the Army that the Gen! Officers have come to an
agreement not to give more than 2 / p! lb. for Butter, & 1 / p! Dozen
for Eggs, & recommends it to them to come to the same Determi-
nation.

Gen! Parson's Brigade & Col? S. B. Webb's Regiment to hold
themselves in readiness to march at the shortest Notice—except
those of Col? Webb's Regiment who have not had the small-pox, of
which there must be a Return made immediately.

There is a number of men more wanted to go in the whale Boats—
those of any Regiment (except what are ordered to march) who are
acquainted with the Water to parade at Head Quarters to-morrow
morning at nine o'clock.

The Regiments are to be brigaded in the following manner,
viz! --

Gen! Nixon's Brigade   Gen! Glovers
   Col? [John] Greaton's   Col? [Rufus] Putnam's
     [William] Shepherds *   Alden's
     [Thomas] Nixon's   Bigelows
     [Edward] Wigglesworth's
Gen! McDougalls   Gen! Huntington's
   Col? [Charles] Webb's   Col. [Henry B.] Livingston's
     [John?] Paterson's   [John] Durkee's
     [Philip Van] Cortlandt's   [Heman] Swift's
     Sam! B. Webb's   [John] Chandler's
Gen! Parsons
   L! Col. [Samuel] Prentice's
       [Col. Samuel] Wyllys's
       [Philip Burr] Bradley's
   L! Col?   Dimons
   Major [Return J.]   Meigs Detachment.

Gen! Glover's & Huntington's Brigades to be commanded by the Senior Officers untill the arrival of the Generals.

The Commanding Officers of each Brigade will order a Return to be made to Head Quarters to-morrow morning.

The Commanding Officer of Gen! Glover's Brigade to appoint some Officer to do the Duty of Brigade Major till further Orders.

HEAD QUARTERS, PEEKSKILL, 13 JUNE, 1777.

Parole, *Boston.*   C. Sign, *Cambridge.*

Col? [Thomas] Nixon   ⎫
Brigade Major ———   ⎬ Officers for to-morrow.
Adjutant   ———   ⎭

Tho the Tour of Duty is properly brigaged Gen! Nixon's,† yet it has (in council held for that purpose) been thought best for particular private Reasons that Brigadier Gen! Parsons should go on Command for the present.

Willm Bialow Esq. is appointed a Deputy Paymaster-Gen! for this Department & is to be obeyed and respected as such.

   * Shepard is also given.

   † Some words probably omitted.

HEAD QUARTERS, PEEKSKILL, 14 JUNE, 1777.

Parole, *Glover.*   C. Sign, *Clinton.*

L! Col. [Isaac] Sherman
B. Major [David] Smith   } Officers for to-morrow.
Adjutant [Peter] Sacket

The Commanding Officers of Regiments & Corps are immediately to make out a Return of the Cloathing & necessaries for their
respective Corps & deliver it to the Gen! .

HEAD QUARTERS, PEEKSKILL, 15 JUNE, 1777.

Parole, *Huntington.*   C. Sign, *Webb.*

The Gen! has thought proper to alter the Arrangement of the
Brigades in the following manner.   Gen! McDougalls & Gen! Glover's Brigades to do Duty till further orders.

Gen! Nixon's Brigade   Gen! McDougall's Brigade
   Col? [Thomas] Nixon's Reg!   Col? Durkee's Reg!
   [Rufus] Putnam's   [Philip Van] Cortlandt's
          Aldens   Chandler's

Gen! Glover's Brigade   Gen! Huntington's Brigade
   Col? Wigglesworth's Reg!   Col. Charles Webb's
   [Wm.] Shepherd's   Paterson's
   [Herman] Swift's   [Henry B.] Livingston's.

A Gen! Court Martial to sit to-morrow morning at 9 o'clock in
the Church to try such prisoners as shall be bro't before them.

Col? Cortlandt, President

L! Col. [Peter] Regnier		Lt.	Waterman
Major	Sumner	˙ Lt.	Obrian
Major	Parks	Lt	Holister
Capt.	Stoddart	Lt	Norton
Capt.	Smith	Lt	Drew
Capt.	Pope	Lt	Felt

(Members.)

M! Smith who has done the Duty of Brigade Major for Comm^d
Livingston's Brigade, to do it for Gen! Huntington's Brigade till
further orders.

HEAD QUARTERS, PEEKSKILL, 16 JUNE, 1777.

Parole, *Griffin.*   C. Sign, *Mifflin.*

Major [Benjamin] Ledyard   ⎫
B. Major [David] Smith   ⎬ Officers for to-morrow.
Adjutant Shipman   ⎭

HEAD QUARTERS, PEEKSKILL, 27 JUNE, 1777.*

Parole, *Huntington.*   C. Sign, *Root.*

L! Col. [Ebenezer] Sproul   ⎫
B. Major Fosdick   ⎬ Officers for to-morrow.
Adjutant Buckmaster   ⎭

1 S. 1 C. 20 P additional for Fatigue to parade to-morrow morning at 6 o'clock to receive Orders from Capt. Buchanan, who will
attend for this Purpose on the Parade. If any Officer is going to
Boston or knows of any Gentleman going there within a Day or two,
they are desired to let Gen! Putnam know of it immediately.

As the Troops in this Department are to be mustered the first of
next Month, Commanding Officers of Companies will immediately
prepare their Muster Rolls to the last day of this Month agreeable
to a form they have received. They will add three whole Columns
(between the Columns of the Soldiers' Inlistment & the Remarks)
to shew the Time for which they are inlisted, whether for the Warr,
three years, or 8 months. Many Officers thro' mistake in the proof
of the Effectives, have blended the Effectives & non Effectives together—such will take Notice, that Dead, Deserted & Discharged
are non Effectives.

If no Commissioned Officer should be present, the non-Commis-

---

* No orders are noted between the 16th and the 27th. General Putnam was
ordered, June 12th, to send forward Generals Parsons, McDougall, and Glover,
with all the Continental troops at Peekskill, except one thousand effective men;
which number, in conjunction with the militia and convalescents at that post, was
deemed equal to the number of the enemy on the east side of the Hudson. The
above detachments were ordered to march in three divisions, each to follow one
day's march behind the other, and each of the first two divisions to be attended
by two pieces of artillery. Platt may have marched with one of the Brigades,
and so lost ten days.

sioned of the Company will make out the Rolls (five in Number) as Exact as possible, and sign them, only it is expected that the Rolls be accurately made out, as none but such can be received. Such Officers as have not been furnished with a form of a Muster Roll, will immediately call upon the Deputy Muster Master at Col? Sam! Drakes for the same.

HEAD QUARTERS, PEEKS KILL, 28 JUNE, 1777.

Parole, *Nixon.*   C. Sign, *Sudbury.*

Major [Warham] Parks

B. Major   Herwood   } Officers for to-morrow.

Adjutant   Convers

Lost the 25th Instant between the Widdow Warren's & Colo [Heman] Swift's Encampment, 32 yards Cotton Linnen 3½ do coarse Linnen & ½ yᵈ blue Velvet, a purple stamp'd pattern for a Vest & 3 Skains thread all wrapt in a Bundle, whoever will bring the same to Cap! Sam! Pell of Col? Cortlandt's Reg!, or to Cap! Jacob Thomas at the Widdow Warren's shall receive 3 Dollars Reward.

The Artillery are immediately to encamp on the Hill back of the Church.

The Chaplains are ordered to attend the Prisoner under Sentence of Death.

HEAD QUARTERS, PEEKS KILL, 29 JUNE, 1777.

Parole, *Massachusetts.*   C. Sign, *Connecticut.*

Col? Shepherd

B. Major [David] Smith   } Officers for to-morrow.

Adjutant [Peter] Sacket

BRIGADE ORDERS, 29 JUNE, 1777.

The Command? Officers of Reg!ˢ & Companies are hereby in-form'd that his Excellency Gen! Washington has ordered that a wagon and four horses be allowed to every hundred men, Officers included. They will therefore regulate the Baggage accordingly,

while they have Leisure, as the Brig^r will not expose himself to the
Gen^{ls} Displeasure, by his Brigade moving with more Carriages than
they are allowed ; nor risque the necessary Baggage of the Brigade
to be lost.   The Tents of every Reg^t will be marked with the Name
of the Col^o to prevent their being lost, or disputes about them.
Such of them as are torn or rotten to be now returned into the
Q^r Mr Gen^{ls} Store.   Whenever the Brigade is ordered to strike Tents
or Decamp, the Tents will be compactly made up without any Poles
or any kind of Baggage within them ; and tied with a String in order
that they be not chaffed.   The Poles also tied & put into a Waggon
under the Tents.   Every Mess will immediately provide themselves
with bark strings sufficient for those purposes.   No Kind of Baggage or Lumber shall be put above the Tents, but Beds or Mattras-
ses.   The Arms of the Brigade will be clean'd & inspected agreeable
to the printed Orders of the 17th May & messed conformable to it.
The Waggon Master will attend at Orderly Hours with the Adjutants.—No Officer or Soldier shall abuse any of the Drivers of the
Brigade, if they neglect their Duty they must be taken prisoners, if
the service will admit or a Complaint entered to the Waggon Master.
On the other Hand the Drivers must attend punctually on their
Duty, the great pay they have, as well as the Common Duty they
owe their Country, loudly calls on them for a faithfull Discharge of
it.   If the motives do not excite them, they will be severely punished.   The Drums & Fifes of the Brigade will practice every morning & afternoon, with the best Drum & fife Majors of the Brigade.
A Return will immediately be made of the Drums & Fifes wanting
in each Reg^t .   The Surgeons of the Brigade will supply themselves
with the necessary Medicines, Dressing & Instruments for their respective Corps ; and make daily Returns of their sick to the Brig^r
& Surgeon Genl of the Army in this Department.   The Brigadier
wishes to see long Orders rendered unnecessary, by every Officer in
the Brigade doing their Duty & promoting Harmony & Love in it,
which are Considerations of vast moment ; in order to our promoting the Service & Interest of our bleeding & distressed Country.
Those who are to mingle their Blood with each other in Defence of
her Common Liberty against one Common Enemy ; should studi-
ously guard against everything that has the least Tendency to create
any uneasiness in the Brigade.   Whoever shall thro imprudence or

otherwise distract that Harmony, so necessary for the Comfort of the Brigade, will be treated as he deserves.

These Orders are not issued from any Apprehension, that there is a Want of Harmony in ye Brigade ; but to preserve it. The Commanding Officers of Regts. will make a Return as soon as possible of the Cloathing due to their Men from the Public & accompany such Return with the Names of the Men, the Company & Regt they belong to, what they have received & what they want opposite to their Names.

HEAD QUARTERS, PEEKS KILL, 30 JUNE, 1777.

Parole, *Sullivan.*   C. Sign, *Greene.*

Lt. Colo [Frederick] Weissenfelts ⎫
Brigade Major [Richard] Platt ⎬ Officers of the day for to-morrow.
Adjutant [Elihu] Marvin   ⎭

All the Troops at this Post are to parade to-morrow morning at nine o'clock on the bald Hill neat & clean to attend the Execution of John Murray.

Genl Nixon's Brigade to be mustered at Peekskill to-morrow morning at 8 o'clock.

HEAD QUARTERS, PEEKS KILL, 1 JULY, 1777.

Parole, *Westfield.*   C. Sign, *Sterling.*

Lt. Colo [Josiah] Starr   ⎫
B. Major [Thomas] Fosdick ⎬ Officers of the day for to-morrow.
Adjutant Marshall   ⎭

HEAD QUARTERS, PEEKS KILL, 2 JULY, 1777.

Parole, *White Plains.*   C. Sign, *Hammon.*

Lt Colo [Giles] Russell   ⎫
B. Major [David] Smith   ⎬ Officers of the day for to-morrow.
Adjutant [Nehemiah] Rice   ⎭

The Gen! Court Martial whereof Col? Nixon was presd! is dissolved.

The Prisoners who have received their Punishment are to be immediately releas'd & sent to their respective Corps.

The Gen! desires Officers will be more careful in future what Prisoners they send to the Provost Guard, as he finds many are confined there for trifling Crimes, properly cognizable by Regimental Courts.

A Gen! Court Martial to sit to-morrow at the Church at 9 o'clock, Col? Wyllys to preside. Majors [Joseph] Hait and [Benjamin] Ledyard, 6 Captains & 4 Subalterns.

Col? [John] Lamb's Battalion of Artillery to be mustered to-morrow afternoon at 4 o'clock. Gen! Huntington's Brigade the morning following at 9 o'clock.

Weekly Returns in future to be delivered at Head Quarters on Friday Mornings at Orderly Time.

HEAD QUARTERS, PEEKS KILL, 3 JULY, 1777.

Parole, *Hannibal.*   C. Sign, *Carthage.*

Major Porter
Brigade Major [Richard] Platt   } Officers of the day for to-morrow.
Adjutant Pearl

BRIGADE ORDERS, 3 JULY, 1777.

As the Main Body of the Enemy's Army may be expected up with the First Wind, the Rolls will be called five Times a Day, immediately after Revellie Beating at 8 in the Morning, at Noon, at 3 in the Afternoon and at retreat Beating. None to leave the Camp without Leave or go without the Sound of the Drum on pain of being punished for a Breach of Orders. Every moment of Time to be improved in manœuvring the Troops.

Such Troops who have lately joined & have not Ammunition, to be immediately furnished with as many Rounds as their Cartouch Boxes will hold. The Ammunition of the Brigades to be examined at 11 o'clock this forenoon, when it will be too hot to exercise.

The Surgeons to provide Bandages & Dressings.

If there is a Deficiency of Arms, the Arms will be put in the Hands of the best Men.

The Brigade to be unincumbered with all Baggage, but such as is absolutely necessary.

The Intrenching Tools to be got to the Camp & delivered into the Care of an Ensign of a Reg! the fullest Officer'd.

The Q! Masters to examine into the State of their Axes & make a Return thereof to the Brigadier this evening, with names of those who have lost any.

HEAD QUARTERS, PEEKS KILL, 4 JULY, 1777.

Parole, *Columbia.*   C. Sign, *Franklin.*

Col? [Edward] Wigglesworth

B. Major [Thomas] Fosdick   } Officers of the Day for to-morrow.

Adjutant Smith

Major Porter with a Hundred Men of Col? Wigglesworth's Reg! properly Officered to march to Fort Constitution to-morrow after mustering.

Gen! Glover's Brigade to be mustered to-morrow morning at 8 o'clock.

HEAD QUARTERS, PEEKS KILL, 5 JULY, 1777.

Parole, *Varnum.*   C. Sign, *Lamb.*

Gen! McDougall's Brigade to be mustered on Monday Morning at 8 o'clock.

None except Commissioned Officers are permitted to take Orders at Head Quarters.

HEAD QUARTERS, PEEKS KILL, 6 JULY, 1777.

Parole, *Jersey.*　　　　　　　　　C. Sign, *Peeks Kill.*

Lt. Colo. [Ebenezer] Sprout　　⎫
B. Major [Richard] Platt　　　⎬ Officers of the day for to-morrow.
Adjutant [Thomas] Convers　　⎭

The Officers of Gen! Parson's Brigade into whose Hands the Boats were delivered, must immediately return them to their respective Station at the Landing.

Benjamin Drake, Serg! in Cap! [Nathan] Strong's Company in Col? Livingston's Reg! tried at a late Gen! Court Martial whereof Col? Wyllys was President, for Desertion.

The Court adjudge & order the Prisoners reduced to the Ranks & to receive Fifty Lashes on his bare back.*

Adam McNeil† of Cap! [Samuel] Sacket's Comp? in Col? Livingston's Reg! tried at the above Court Martial for not joining the Regiment & inlisting twice.

The Court considering the Circumstances of the Prisoner, sentence him to receive fifty Lashes upon the naked [back].

Elihu Brown of Cap! Goodale's Comp? , Col? [Rufus] Putnam's Reg! tried at the same Court, for Desertion & forging a Pass in the Name of Major Newell.

The Court adjudge the Prisoner guilty of forging a pass, which together with the Crime of Desertion, the Court sentence him to receive one Hundred Lashes upon his bare back.

John Obrian private ‡ in Col? Cortlandt's Reg! tried at the same Court, for stealing Liquor & getting drunk, sleeping on his Post, & absenting himself from his Guard. The Court is of opinion that there has been no sufficient Proof of the Prisoner's stealing liquor ; but for the other Charges against him, sentence him to receive fifty Lashes on his bare back.

The Gen! approves the several Sentences and orders them to be put in Execution to-morrow Morning at the usual Time & Place, ex-

* There was a Benoni Drake in Captain Strong's Company, who deserted in November, 1777.

† In Volume of Rolls this is given McKeal.

‡ In the Company of Captain Charles Graham.

cept that, respecting Serg! Drake. He is pleased to forgive the Lashes, considering his long Confinement ; but orders him to join his Company as a private & be studious to avoid any future Misdemeanors, as he may rely on being treated with severe justice.

A Board of Gen! Officers to sit to-morrow morning at 8 o'clock at the Widdow Warren's, to examine the Pretensions & settle the Rank of the Field Officers from the State of Connecticut.

Considering the present Urgency, the Gen! directs that the Artificers continue the necessary Business of the Army, even on Sundays unless particularly instructed to the Contrary.

The Gen! is resolved to prevent the small Pox from spreading among the Troops or Militia who are arriving. For this Purpose all Officers & Soldiers who appear to be infected shall be immediately removed to the small pox Hospital, & nowhere else. He expects the Officers will exert themselves for the exact Observance of this Order & he assures them that every infected Person who presumes to go more than a Hundred Yards from the small Pox Hospital without a Certificate from the Surgeon, that he is sufficiently cleans'd, shall be treated [as] a Common Enemy, be the Consequences ever so fatal.

BRIGADE ORDERS, 6 JULY, 1777.

It will give the Brigadier great pleasure to find the men wash themselves early in the morning & late in the afternoon ; but such as shall be found in the Mill pond or Creek from 8 o'clock in the Morning till six in the Evening strip'd will be punished as violators of Orders. The Adjutants will be answerable, that this Order be read to every Comp͡y in their respective Regiments.

A Captain will be appointed every Day to inspect into the State of the Camp & report it to the Brigadier. He will call on him for particular Orders every Day at 8 o'clock in the Morning. No Officer shall presume to give furloughs to any Officer or Soldier of the Brigade, without leave in writing from the Brigadier.

HEAD QUARTERS, PEEKS KILL, 7 JULY, 1777.

Parole, *Courtland*.   C. Sign, *Bergen*.

Col? [William] Shepherd
B. Major [Thomas] Fosdick } Officers of the day for to-morrow.
Adjutant [Elihu] Marvin

The Colonels & Commanding Officers of Corps to make a Return to Head Quarters immediately of the Surgeons & Mates of their respective Corps, whether they are in Camp or absent, and if absent, on what Duty.

The Regimental Surgeons, or in their absence the States are to make daily Returns to Doctor Burnet the Surgeon General of what Number of sick they have under their Care & their Disorder.

HEAD QUARTERS, 8 JULY, 1777.

Parole, *Root*.   C. Sign, *Branch*.

By Accounts from New York the Enemy are making preparation for a movement, it is expected that they will come up this way. The Gen! therefore requests that the Commanding Officers of Regiments will see that their Arms are in good Order ; and that they are properly Equiped otherways, so as to be able to turn out on the Shortest Notice.

There is plenty of Ammunition if any is wanted ; immediate Application should be made : that there may be no excuse in case of an Alarm.

The Guards in future are to come on the parade precisely at 6 o'clock in the morning, or the Brigade Major to suffer the Consequence in Case of any Neglect.

HEAD QUARTERS, MIDDLETOWN, 1 JULY, 1777.

His Excellency Gen! Washington has been pleased to appoint Thomas Fosdick, Esq., Brigade Major (to the Brigade commanded by Brigadier-General Glover) and he is to be respected and obeyed as such.

HEAD QUARTERS, PEEKS KILL, 7 JULY, 1777.

Parole, *Lookout.*   C. Sign, *Sharp.*

Lt. Col? [Josiah] Starr   ⎫
B. Major [Richard] Platt   ⎬ Officers for to-morrow.
Adjutant [Thomas] Converse   ⎭

If any Reg! in Camp has a Barber to spare, the Commanding Officer is desired to send him to Head Quarters.

Tried at a Gen! Court Martial of which Col? [Samuel] Wyllys was President.

Wm. Ross of Cap! [James] Eldridge's Com? late Col? [Jedidiah] Huntington's Regiment, for attempting to desert to the Enemy. The Court sentence the Prisoner to receive one Hundred Lashes upon the naked back.

John Wilds of Cap! [Martin] Kirtland's Company, late Col? [William] Douglass's Reg! , for desertion the second time. The Court having no proof before it of the First Desertion ; but for the Crime against the Prisoner of Desertion the second time, sentence s? Prisoner to receive one Hundred Lashes on his bare back.

John Thompson of Cap! [John] Mills Com? , Col? Charles Webb's Regiment, tryed for deserting from & inlisting into three Different Reg!s and taking Continental Bounty.

The Court considering the Circumstances of the Prisoner being an old and worthless person, sentence him to receive one hundred lashes and then to be drum'd out of Camp with a Halter about his Neck as a Rogue and Rascall.

The Gen! approves the above sentences and orders them to be executed to-morrow Morning at Guard Mounting, at which time all the Drums & fifes in Camp will attend the Grand parade, and if he is ever seen in Camp to be treated as a Common Enemy to the United States.

The Cattle and Sheep that were taken by Col? Courtland at Bergen to be sold at publick Vendue to-morrow at ten o'clock on the Grand Parade. If any Gentlemen chose to take them at the Apprisal they must appear.

A Serg!s Guard to mount at Barracks No. 3. No men except such as have had the small pox to mount the above. The Serg! to take Directions from the Surgeon General or his Assistants.

The Gen! C. Martial of which Col? [Samuel] Wyllys was president
is dissolved.

Major [Warham] Park[s], Capts Tuckerman & Pope to inspect
the Provisions at Commissarys Store and report to the Gen! immediately such as is not fit for use in Order that it may not be condemned.

After Orders.

Jesse Root, Esq., is appointed Deputy A. Gen! for this Department and is to be obeyed and respected accordingly.

HEAD QUARTERS, PEEKS KILL, 10 JULY, 1777.

Parole, *Leonard.*   C. Sign, *Webb.*

L! Col? [Giles] Russel
B. Major [Thomas] Fosdick   } Officers of the day for to-morrow.
Adjutant Smith

The Gen! orders the Disposition of the several Brigades to be as
follows, viz! :—

Brigadier Gen! McDougall's Brigade to be on the Right near the
old Orchard.

B. Gen! Parsons on the Left between H! Quarters and Col?
Sam! Drake's.

B. Gen! Varnum's on the right of the Center next to Gen! Mc-
Dougall's.

B. Gen! Glover's on the left of the Center next to Gen! Parsons.

B. Gen! Huntington's in the center upon the Fish Kill road leading from Peeks Kill.

Two Cannon to be fixed at the forts Independance, Montgomery
& Constitution.

The above Sentence should a come in after the next below.

The Signal to be given on the appearance of the Enemy is firing
of two Cannon from Gen! Varnum one Minute from each other, two
ditto at the park by Gen! Huntington two D? by Gen! Parsons in
like Manner.

The Brigades to be as follows, viz! :—

Col? [John] Durkee's
Col? [Philip Van] Cortland's   } Gen! McDougall's.
Col? [John] Chandler's

Col? Charles Webb's
Col? [Samuel] Prentice's
Col? [Samuel] Wyllys's   } Gen! Parsons'
   [David] Dimond's

Col? S. Green's
Col? S[amuel B.] Webb's
Col? [Henry] Sherburne's   } Gen! Varnum's
Col? [Israel] Angel's

Col? [Joseph] Vose's
Col? [Edward] Wigglesworth's } Gen! Glover's
Col? [William] Shepherd's

Col? [Philip Burr] Bradley's
Col? [Heman] Swift's   } Gen! Huntington's
Col? [Henry B.] Livingston's

HEAD QUARTERS, PEEKS KILL, 11 JULY, 1777.

Parole, *England.*   C. Sign, *America.*

Col? [Edward] Wigglesworth
B. Major McDougall   } Officers of the day for to-morrow.
Adjutant Pearl.

The Gen! considering the Busy Season of the Year & how import-
ant it is to the public as well as to themselves that the Militia be at
home in their Business at this Time, & not being now wanted, altho'
he cannot say how soon they may be—The three Reg!s of Militia viz!
Col⁰ˢ [Cornelius] Humphrey's, [Henry] Luddington's, & [Derck]
Brinkerhoff's, who first came in are dismissed with the Gen!s thanks
for their Alertness in coming to the Defence of their Country when
desired & for their good Services relying upon it that the Zeal &
Ardor they have shewn in the great Cause we are engaged in, will
prompt them to turn out without (*sic*) the utmost Alacrity on all
future Occasions.

Col? [Samuel] Wyllys's & [William] Douglass's Reg!s are to meet
to attend prayers at five o'clock to-morrow Morning. Divine Service
will be perform'd here by the Reverend Doctor [Abiel] Leonard
next Lord's Day.

Fifty men to parade to-morrow morning at five o'clock without arms with the party ordered to Fort Montgomery to go on Fatigue with two Subalterns.

The Muster Master acquaints such Officers as have not delivered in their Muster Rolls properly attested that he will be under the Necessity of making out his Regimental Abstracts without inserting them unless they are immediately sent in.

HEAD QUARTERS, PEEKS KILL., 12 JULY, 1777.

Parole, *Windsor.*   C. Sign, *Park.*

Mʳ George Havens is appointed Conductor of Ordnance Stores at Fort Montgomery & the other Posts in the Highlands, in the Room of the Conductor * who is appointed an Officer in Colᵒ [William] Malcom's Regᵗ .

The Genᴸ is sorry that no more attention is paid to the Preservation of the Forage—orders that no Officer or Soldier in future will take any Forage or Feed by turning in Horses, belonging to private property, without first applying to the Qʳ Mʳ or Forage Master to have the same assigned him & such Qʳ Master &c. after finding where it may be had is to report the same to the Genᴸ for his liberty, before any such forage or feed may be taken or horses turned in.

Lᵗ Colᵒ [David] Dimon
B. Major [David] Humphreys } Officers of the day for to-morrow.
Adjutant Selden

HEAD QUARTERS, 13 JULY, 1777.

Parole, *Boston.*   C. Sign, *Cambridge.*

Roger Alden, Esqʳ , is appointed to act as B. Major to Brigᵗ Genᴸ Huntington's Brigade till further orders & is to be respected & obeyed accordingly.

* Probably Daniel Neven (or Nivins), commissioned a Captain in Malcom's Regiment, 2 July, 1777.

HEAD QUARTERS, PEEKS KILL, 14 JULY, 1777.

Lt. Col? [Matthew] Mead
B. Major [Roger] Alden   } Officers of the day for to-morrow.
Adjutant Barker

As Health & a respectable Appearance among Officers & Soldiers gives Strength & Dignity to an Army—and as their keeping themselves clean & neat, using proper diet well dress'd & not lying on the cold ground, & in the damp night air needlessly will contribute much to the Preservation of their Health & the Dignity of their Appearance. The Gen! expects that the Troops keep themselves clean & neat, their Hair cut decently short & comb'd & avoid using unwholesome Food or that is partially cook'd, when they have opportunity to cook it thoroughly. Also that they take Care not to lye upon the cold ground or in the damp night air when the Situation of the Army doth not make it necessary. And if any of the Officers should be so inattentive to the Preservation of their Health & Reputation as to neglect to observing these Regulations—the Gen! requests the Officers to exert their Influence by Authority & by Example to compel & induce the Soldiers to a Compliance therewith & to inspire them with every Military Virtue.

A Brigadier General of the Day will be appointed to whom Returns are to be made & by whom Complaints are to be heard & Examinations taken, who is to direct in Regulating the Affairs of the Camp & to Command in the absence of the Gen! .

The Commanding Officers of Companies at the daily Roll Calling to examine the Arms & Ammunition of the men in their respective Companies, see that they are well equipt & that they do not waste their Ammunition, note & report the Deficiencies that in case of an attack from the Enemy, we may be ready to meet them.

A Gen! Court Martial to sit to-morrow morning at 9 o'clock at the Widdow Warren's to try such prisoners as shall be bro't before them. Col? [William] Shepherd to preside. Majors [Ebenezer] Grey & [Thomas] Grosvenor,

1 C. 1 S. from Gen! McDougall's Brigade
2   1   from Gen! Parson's   do   } Members
0   2   from Gen! Huntington's do
1   2   from Gen! Varnum's   do

HEAD QUARTERS, PEEKS KILL, 15 JULY, 1777.

Brig.̲ Gen.̲ McDougall
Lt. Col.̲ [Isaac] Sherman
Major [Thomas] Fosdick
Adj.̲ Learned } Officers of the Day.

As nothing renders an Army so formidable to the Enemy, so respectable & usefull to its friends & so internally secure in itself as being expert in War—at this Time when we expect daily to be ingaged and the ordinary Camp Duty but small, the Gen.̲ expects the Troops that are of [f] Duty will be employed in Military Exercises, & directs that every Company shall be exercised from Revellie Beating to six o'clock in the Morning the Time of Relieving Guards, & from 8 o'clock to ten in the Forenoon & from 4 o'clock in the afternoon till seven & that each Reg.̲ shall have two field Days in a Week for Regimental Exercises,̍ those of B. Gen.̲ McDougall's on Monday's & Thursday's, those of B. Gen.̲ˢ Parsons', Varnum's, Glover's, & Huntington's on Tuesday's & Friday's.

The Season of the year being hot & unhealthy & the Time draws nigh, in which we may expect the Enemy will begin their Capital Operations when our whole strength may be wanted, the Gen.̲ strictly prohibits all persons from taking or communicating the small pox by Inoculation or in any other voluntary Manner under the severest penalties.

The Gen.̲ orders that the Q.̲ M.̲ provide & deliver to the Troops slings for their Canteens, Bayonet Belts.

At a Gen.̲ Court Martial held at Phillipsburgh on Sunday, July 13ᵗʰ, 1777, by order of Philip Van Cortlandt.

L.̲ Col.̲ [Frederick] Weissenfels, President.

Thomas Powall private in Capt. [Charles] Graham's C.̲ Col.̲ Cortlandt's Reg.̲ was tried for Deserting to the Enemy returning & deserting again & persuading other Soldiers to desert with him, found guilty & sentenced to be shot to Death. The Gen.̲ approves the Sentence, & orders it to be executed on Monday next the 21ˢᵗ of this Instant between the Hours of ten & Eleven in the Morning.

B. Gen.̲ Parson's Brigade hath Liberty to discharge their Pieces at Retreat Beating this Evening under the Directions of their Officers.

The Bridge Guard to be augmented to 30 privates.

Lost on the Road from White Plains the day before yesterday, a large leather pocket Book, Sam! Brown wrote on it, two 30 Doll! Bills, three 1/ N York Bills, one 6ᵈ Do a number of papers—if the Pocket Book should be found, it is ordered to be bro't to Head Quarters.

HEAD QUARTERS, PEEKS KILL, 16 JULY, 1777.

Brigad! Gen! Parsons
Col? S. B. Webb   } Officers of the Day.
Brigade Major [David] Humphreys
Adjutant Hopkins.

The Gen! having been informed of Damage being done to private property by the Soldiers destroying the Fences, &c. strictly forbid the Troops taking away or burning any Fence or rails to the Detriment of any particular Inclosure & expects that the Officers will take special care that this order is observed.

Taken from Thomas Smith, Esq! , a pint silver porringer yesterday, the Handle had carv'd work upon it with a Hole in the End of it on the Back of the Porringer were the Letters T. C. T. Any persons finding sᵈ porringer are to Convey it to Col? Livingston or to Hᵈ Qʳˢ & shall receive an Honorable Reward.

Col? [Philip Burr] Bradley's Reg! has Liberty to discharge their pieces this Evening at Retreat Beating under the Direction of their Officers.

HEAD QUARTERS, PEEKS KILL, 17 JULY, 1777.

Gen! Varnum,
L! Col? Olney   } Officers of the Day to-morrow.
B. Major [Richard] Platt
Adj! [John] Holden [Jr.]

The Gen! orders a Picquet Guard at the Church near King's Ferry to consist of 1 M. 2 C. 4 S. 8 S. 8 C. 2 DF. 120 P. to mount this Evening & to be relieved to-morrow Morning. That the Detail for Guards & Fatigue be taken from all the Brigades indifferently—that special Care be taken to receive & communicate Gen! Orders to the Troops by the Officers, for the Plea of Ignorance is inadmissible to excuse.

The Picquet above ordered is to keep Patrols consisting of twelve men each, continually out patroling down the River & towards Croton to make Discoveries, & to take any Scouts from the Enemy & to Kill all tory Villains found in arms against their Country or plundering or carrying any Cattle or Goods to the Enemy & such patroles are strictly forbid to plunder or injure the Inhabitants being quietly in their Business on any Pretence whatever as they must answer it at their Peril.

The Gen! orders that the Troops have special Regard to the Preservation of their Health, now the season is approaching in which it is usually sickly in Camp owing partly to the Season ; but more to their own Imprudence.

That the Troops avoid eating unripe Fruit, going into swimming, drinking too freely of cold water when they are hot & their blood inflam'd.

At a Gen! Court Martial holden by Order of the Gen! 16th July, 1777, Col? [William] Shepherd, President.

David Hass of Capt. Ball's C? in Col? Shepherd's Regt. was tried for Desertion & acquitted.

William Gordon of Capt. [Samuel] Sacket's Compy in Col? [Henry B.] Livingston's Regt. was tried for Desertion & inlisting into another Regt. found guilty & sentenced to receive 100 Lashes upon his Naked back.

John Whiting, alius Jo Wright in Capt. Blusdale's Company, Col? [Edward] Wigglesworth's Regt. was tried for inlisting twice, viz! in Col? Durkee's Regt. after he had inlisted in Col? Wigglesworth's found guilty & sentenced to receive 100 Lashes on his naked back.

Nathaniel Please of Capt. Ball's Compy in Col? [William] Shepherd's Regt. was tried for Desertion, found guilty & sentenced to receive 100 Lashes on his naked back.

The Gen! approves the sentence of the Court Martial respecting the several Prisoners afore said & orders the same to be executed to-morrow morning at Guard Mounting.

A Party for fatigue to consist of 1 C. 3 S. 4 S. 4 C. 50 P. to parade to-morrow morning at Guard Mounting with three Day's provisions.

Major Hait Field Officer of the Picquet to-night & Major Sill Field Officer for to-morrow.

BRIGADE ORDERS, 18 JULY, 1777.

The Brigade will practise the Manual & Manœuvres ordered by
the King of Great Britain in 1764, for his Army till it shall be otherwise ordered by the Commander in Chief. Such Officers as have
not practised in Exercise & Manœuvres will be industrious in per-
fecting themselves : as the Brigadier intends calling on every Commissioned Officer of the Brigade to exercise & manœuvre the respective Reg^ts to which they belong. Those Officers who are practised in those particulars will drill the awkward Serg^ts to qualify them
to drill the Rank & File. The Sergeants, Rank & File of every Regiment will provide themselves with a hard stick of the size & form of
a Cartridge & keep them in their pouches to go thro' the firing
motions.

*   *   *   *   *   *

Edmund Palmer that Noted Tory a Robber Was taken Prisoner
& Confined in ye Provost Guard for Robing the Inhabitence & Lev-
ing war Against his Country : is to have his Tryal Next Tuesday at
9 o'clock in the Morning by A General Court Marshel all Parsons
that Can give Evidence Against s^d Palmer are Requested & Required
to Attend the Trial.*

HEAD QUARTERS July ye 19th 1777.

Brigadier General [Jedidiah] Huntington ⎫
Colo [John] Chandler † ⎬ Officers of the Day.
Adj^t [Henry] Ten Eyck ⎭

The general orders *all Sutlers and* the Sellers of Stores in Camp
Except ye Comisarys of Particular Brigades (*States*) Who are Appointed to Deal out the State Stores to their own Troop at Perticulir
(*certain*) Prices (*immediately*) to make a Return to him of their
Names of ye Quantity & Quality of th[e] Goods the Prices they Sell
at and By what author[ity] they (*suttle*) Settle In Camp. Capt [Eb-
enezer] Flagg is appointed to Act as Brigade Magor to *Brigadier*

---

* This paragraph, the first of the entries in Sergeant Ware's book, is not found
in Platt's.

† Of the Eighth Regiment, Connecticut Line.

General Varnams Brigade till further orders and is to be *respected
and* obayd as Such   A bourd of General officers to set on Munday
Next *at 9 o'clock in the morning* at yᵉ house of the Widow Warrens
to Enquire into the (*Pretensions and*) Perticular Clames of Several
Candidates of the Late Vacant officers of the Late Col [William]
Douglas* Who is Deceased & of the Regᵗ Lately Commanded by
Colo [Jedidiah] Huntington Who is Promoted and Report to (*the
Honorable*) Magor General Putnam with their appinian of the Prem-
esis in order to Be Transmited to gena[l] Washington yᵉ sᵈ Board
to Consist of Generals Mc : Dougle Varnam (*Glover*) & Huntington

a Court of inquirey to Set Next Munday at 9 ocl[ock] in yᵉ morning to Inquire into the Several Cri[mes] of the Prisoners in the
Provost Guard the nature & Evidence theirof & make Report of
that they Shall Find with there oppinian Respecting them

the Court of Inquirey Colo [Heman] Swift, Capt Hide [Jedidiah
Hyde] Capt Mattuck [Samuel Mattocks] Capᵗ [John] Harmon

A full C[aptˢ] Company

1 Capᵗ	4 Sargᵗ 4 Corpˡ
2 Lieutenants	2 Drum & Fife & [ ]
1 Ensign	Privates †

are ordered to be Detachd from Colo. [Philip Burr] Bradleys Regiment to goe to Fort Independance & Releave the Melitia at t[hat]
Post tomorrow

Brigadier General Huntington ⎫
Colonel [John] Chandler   ⎬ Officers of the day to-morrow.
Brigade Major [Ebenezer] Flagg ⎪
Adjutant [Henry] Teneik   ⎭

HEAD QUARTERS, PEEKS KILL, 20 JULY, 1777.

Lost yesterday a Pᵗ of Sadle Baggs near Hᵈ Qʳˢ with Men's Clothes
& Linnen in them, any Person that shall find sᵈ Baggage with the
Cloathing & deliver them at Hᵈ Qʳˢ shall be well rewarded.

* "*Claims of the several candidates for the office of Colonel in the Regᵗ late
Douglass's.*"—*Platt.*   Douglass died of hard service, 28 May, 1777.

† In Platt's record, the figures differ from these.

HEAD QUARTERS, PEEKS KILL, 21 JULY, 1777.

Brigadier General Varnum
Lt. Col. [Giles] Russell
Brigade Major ———
Adjutant ———

The Picquet at the Church is reduced to 1 C, 2 S, 4 S, 4 C, 2 D. F., 50 P.

Lt. Col? [Jeremiah] Olney & Major [Samuel] Ward are appointed Members of the Court Martial of which Col? Shepherd is Pres! — one Cap! & one Subaltern from Gen! McDougall's Brigade, one Cap! & 2 Subalterns from Gen! Glover's Brigade to supply the vacancies occasioned by the Marching of Gen! Parson's & Huntington's Brigades.

1 S, 15 P. that are reapers to parade at Head Quarters to-morrow Morning with Sickles from General Glover's Brigade.

A dark rone Horse taken up by Major [Joseph] Hait in Camp as a stray ; the owner on applying may have him.

Colonel [John] Chandler is appointed President of the Court of Enquiry upon the Prisoners in the Provost Guard in the place of Colo. [Heman] Swift. S? Court to sit to-morrow morning at nine o'clock.

———

HEAD QUARTERS, 22ND JULY, 1777.

Parole, *Newark.*   Countersign, *Elizabeth.*

Brigadier Genl Glover
Col? [Joseph] Vose   } Officers of the Day.
B. Major [Ebenezer] Flagg
Adjutant Pearl

The Picquet kept at the Church in future is to be taken from Lord Sterling's Division, consisting of one field officer & 120 men as at first.

The Court appointed to examine into the Grounds of Uneasiness among the Commissioned Officers of Col? [Edward] Wigglesworth's Reg! occasioned by the appointment of Major Porter, report that as Major Porter was appointed by authority which was proper and competent for the Purpose, it ought not to be drawn into Question by them.

The Gen! approves the Sentence & earnestly recommends it to all Officers of the Army not to let trifling Considerations respecting Prudence [precedence ?] & Rank impede or divert their Attention from the great Object for which we are at War, viz. the Defence & Salvation of our Country, remembering that true Honor results not so much from Elevation of Rank & Place as from Sublimity of Soul & great military exploits.

At a Gen! Court Martial held by order of the Honᵇˡᵉ Major Gen! Putnam at Peekskill on the 17th Instant, Colº Shepherd, President.

The following Soldiers were tried for the several Crimes annexed to their Names respectively, viz :

Amos Rose, private in Colo. Sam! B. Webb's Regᵗ tried for firing a gun loaded with a Ball at Lt. [Elisha] Brewster, found guilty & sentenced to suffer the Pains of Death.

The Gen! approves the Sentence & orders that said Rose be shot to Death on Friday the first of next August between the Hours of Ten & Eleven in the Morning.

Henry Hercules Hoff, private in Colº [Henry B.] Livingston's Regᵗ tried at the above Court for Desertion, found guilty & sentenced to receive one Hundred Lashes on his naked back.

Sam! Fosdick of Colº Livingston's Regᵗ tried by sᵈ Court for Desertion, found guilty, & sentenced to receive 50 Lashes on his naked back.

Thoˢ Doyle tried by sᵈ Court for Desertion, found guilty & sentenced to receive 100 Lashes on his naked back.

Thoˢ Colvill of Colo. Sam! B. Webb's Regᵗ tried by sᵈ Court for Desertion, found guilty & sentenced to receive 50 Lashes on his naked back.

Edward Murphey of Lᵗ Colº [Jeremiah] Olney's Detachment tried for Desertion found guilty & sentenced to receive 100 Lashes on his naked back.

Henry Williams of Colº [Heman] Swift's Regᵗ tried for perswading Soldiers to desert, found guilty & sentenced to receive 100 Lashes on his naked Back.

The Gen! approves the several Sentences & orders them to be executed to-morrow morning at Guard Mounting on the grand parade.

The Gen! is sorry that he is so frequently put to the disagreeable Necessity of ordering Punishments to be inflicted owing to the great

Frequency of Crimes, the Perpetration of which renders punishments absolutely necessary for the Reformation of Offenders, & to
deter others in order to maintain that Subordination, Order & Reg-
ularity which is necessary for the well-being of an Army—earnestly
recommends it to all the Soldiers to take Warning by the Sufferings
of others : for tho his Eye pities their Sufferings, his justice will not
spare their Crimes, & so to behave as to give as little Occasion for
the disagreeable Employment of inflicting punishment as possible &
to prevent what he imagines to be one principle cause of such ir-
regular Conduct, viz! drinking spirituous Liquors to Excess, he
strictly forbids the Soldiers frequenting taverns, Tippling Houses, or
Sutler's Shops where spirituous Liquors are sold & their drinking
spirituous Liquors to excess.

The Provost Guard is augmented to 1 C., 2 S., 2 S, 2 C, 2 D. F.,
50 P.

Gen! McDougall's Brigade hath Liberty to discharge their Pieces
this Evening at Retreat Beating under the Direction of their
Officers.

After Orders, 22 July, 1777.

Considering the Imperfection of Man & his liability to err ; The
Inexperience & Rashness of Youth that betrays them into many
criminal Imprudences & exposes often to be seduced into evil prac-
tices by the Example of false pretence & subtle Insinuations of de-
signing Veterans in Iniquity & that in some Cases where it would be
perfectly just to inflict punishment, the great End of Government
will be answered, the Public Interest Secured by the Exercise of
Mercy in the forgiveness of offenders—trusting that all these Reasons concur in the present case to urge & justify the Hand of Clemency in being reached out to save two unhappy young men who are
justly condemned for their Crimes & trembling with the anticipation
of their Punishment just ready to come upon them—

It is the Genl! good Pleasure that Sam! Fosdick & Thos. Colvin
receive a pardon & a Pardon is hereby granted to each of them &
it is ordered that they be discharged without receiving Punishments
& join their Reg!s, relying upon It that the Consideration of this
Goodness to them will more Strongly induce them to virtuous &
order Behavior than the Smart & Twinges of Punishment. At the
same time would caution every one against taking Encouragement
from this act of Clemency to presume to transgress.

CAMP AT FRADRICKS BOROUGH JULY 22 1777

Brigade orders for genaral Parsones Brigade : the General Expects that ye officers take Perticuler Care that no Ingury be Done to Indeviduals under Pretence of their being Enemys to the Cause We are ingaged in and there be no Complaints in Camp or on ye March of fences being Destroyd or any Damage being Commited by the Soldiers of the Brig[ade] the Roles of ye Respective Companys are to be Calld [   ] Every Day : viz Morning & Evening at Which time the Commisiond officers When off Duty are Expected to Att[end] 1 Capt. 2 Subaltons 4 Sarg^{ts} 4 Cor^l. & 50 Privates are to Parade tomorrow at 1 oclock at ye Church with three Days Provision.

CAMP AT FRADRACKS BOROUGH Y^E 23^D JULY 1777

Regimental orders the Reg^t to Perade Dayly for Exercise Agreeable to the general & Brigade orders Captains & officers Commanding Company are to Make their Pay abstracts for Six Months to ye Pay master Without Delay to Make an Abstract for Each Month Seperately tho officers of the Day for ye Camp [will?] be for the futuer Mentioned in orders : No one is to Stray Any Distance from Camp Without Leave all the Lasure time ye men have Should Be Spent in Brightning their arms till they git them Very Bright and Clean   Strict attention ought to be Paid * the Teems Which Brought provisions from thence May be Made use of for that purpose   Such Inverleads as are Scattered on ye Road the general Directs should be Collected together that an attentive and Prudent officer from Each Reg^t Be Sent to take ye Charge of them & Bring on By Easy Marches Such as are able to join ye Brigade

a guard from Each Reg^t to Be kept to Prevent ye horses or oxen Straying or Being Stole or Breaking into Inclosiers & Doing unnessary Damage   the unavoidable Destruction an army Makes in its Progress is But two great without ye aditional Evil of Criminal Neglegence for Wanton Depradations [He] Would fondly flatter him Self of the Fealings of h[uma]nity and ye Dictates of honour as to Become Plunderers and Villians as to Subject them Selves to [   ] & Punishment and Loose the fare Rep[utation] they have Alredy aquired to Presarve [   ] Carrecter will Ever give E^m the greatest Pleasure and Satisfaction

* Some words omitted.

HEAD QUARTERS, PEEKS KILL, 23 JULY, 1777.

Parole, *Goshen.*   C. Sign, *Kent.*

Brig? Gen! McDougall
L! Col? [Henry B.] Livingston   ⎫
B. Major [Thomas] Fosdick   ⎬ Officers of the Day to-morrow.
Adjut! Larnard   ⎭

The Gen! strictly forbids all persons robbing Gardens or taking
any thing from the Inhabitants without leave of the Owner's or
wasting or destroying private property of any kind, whereby the Inhabitants may be injured or distress'd on pain of severe punishment
& all officers are strictly enjoined to see that this order is observed
& complied with.

HEAD QUARTERS, PEEKS KILL, 24 JULY, 1777.

Parole, *Sterling.*   C. Sign, *Durkee.*

Brigadier Gen! Varnum   ⎫
Major [Samuel] Ward   ⎬ Officers of the Day.
Brigade Major [Ebenezer] Flagg   ⎪
Adjutant [John] Remington   ⎭

Gen! Glover's Brigade is ordered to march to the Northward to
join our Army there with all Expedition.

A Fatigue Party of Reapers from Gen! McDougall's Brigade of
1 S, 1 S., 1 C., 20 P. to parade at Head Quarters to-morrow morning to have fatigue Rum & Wages.

Major [Ebenezer] Huntington 1 C., 3 S, 4 S, 4 C, 4 D. F., 100
P. to relieve the garrison at Fort Constitution to-morrow morning.

Col? S. B. Webb's Reg! hath Liberty to discharge their Pieces this
Evening at Retreat Beating under the Direction of their Officers.

At a Gen! Court Martial held at Peeks Kill by order of the
Hon'ble Major Gen! Putnam, 22 July, 1777, Colonel [William]
Shepherd, President.

Serg! John Smith & William White of Cap! D. Dexter's Company,
Col? Angel's Reg! were tried for Desertion & attempting to go to
the Enemy, for stealing & embezzling Cartridges & carrying off their
Arms & accoutrements belonging to the Continent.

The Court find the Prisoners guilty & sentence the Serg!ᵗˢ to be reduced to the Ranks & each of them to receive 100 Lashes on their naked backs.

The Gen! approves the sentence & orders it to be executed to [morrow] morning at Guard Mounting.

Edmund Palmer was arraigned & tried upon a Charge of Plundering, robbing & carrying off Cattle, Goods, &c. from the well-affected Inhabitants & for being a Spy for the Enemy.*

The Court finds him guilty of the whole Charge alledged against him, & sentence him to suffer the Pains of Death.

The Gen! approves the Sentence & orders it to be put in Execution on Fryday, the 1st. of next August ensuing between the Hours of 9 & 11 in the Morning—by hanging him up by the Neck till he is dead, dead, dead.

Jeremiah Maybee was bro't before the Court on suspicion of being a Spy.

The Court find him to be an Inhabitant of this State & his Offence of such a Nature, that its proper to refer him to the Convention or civil Authority of this State.

L! John Waterman & Ensign Abbit [John Abbot] of Colo. Durkee's Reg! were bro't to Trial upon an Arrest by order of Col? Phillip Cortlandt for behaving in a scandalous & cowardly manner before the Enemy on a scouting Party near the White Plains on the 10th Instant & making a false Alarm in Quarters at the same time.

The Court upon maturely considering the case adjudge Lt. Waterman guilty of behaving in a scandalous and Cowardly Manner before the Enemy; but are of opinion that he did not wilfully occasion a false Alarm in Quarters & thereupon order that s? Waterman be cashiered & that his Crime, Name, Place of Abode & Punishment be published in the news paper in & about the Camp and in that State, from whence he came & where he usually resided—but as for the s? Charge against s? Abbit they are of Opinion that he is not guilty & acquit him with Honor.

The Gen! approves the Sentences & orders s? Waterman to quit his Reg! & the Army forthwith.†

* The proceedings of the Court Martial are printed in *Calendar of New York Historical Manuscripts*, II, 258.

† Abbot resigned in December, 1777.

John Smith, William White & Doctor Taller's Negro are ordered to be sent on board the Men of Warr immediately upon receiving their Punishments at Fort Montgomery.

The Person in whose Hands the marking Iron is, will return it to Head Quarters immediately.

HEAD QUARTERS, PEEKS KILL, 25 JULY, 1777.

Parole, *Crane.*   C. Sign, *Lamb.*

The following is an order issued at Head Quarters, Ramapaugh, 23ᵈ Inst :—

The March of the Army whenever it begins will be made with the utmost Dispatch. This renders it indispensably necessary to divest it of as much Baggage as possible.

Each Brigadier is therefore immediately to cause certain Waggons to be prepared for the Tents of his Brigade, and when Orders are given to march they are to suffer nothing to be put into these Waggons but the Tents & see that they are not heavy loaded even with them—& the more to facilitate the march of the Army, the Commissaries are to leave no Means untried to procure a Supply of hard Bread to be reserved for the march—& when the Army moves they are to go forward before it & get the Provisions ready to be delivered out the moment the Army halts. The Qʳ Mʳ Genˡ will have ready a proper Number of empty Waggons to follow each Brigade to take up the sick & lame. The rest of the Baggage is to be left under the Care of a small Guard to follow on after the Army accompanied by the women—None of them are to be suffered to go with the Troops.

12 Seamen to parade to-morrow morning to go on board the Boats under Capᵗ Buchanan.

HEAD QUARTERS, PEEKS KILL, 26 JULY, 1777.

Parole, *Kingston.*   C. Sign, *Princeton.*

Brigᵗ Genˡ Varnum
Lt. Colᵒ [Jeremiah] Olney
B. Major [Ebenezer] Flagg   } Officers of the day.
Adjutant [John] Holden [Jr.]

A Genˡ Court Martial to sit at the Widdow Warren's at 9 o'clock next Monday Morning. Colᵒ Durkee to sit as President. 3 Capᵗˢ & 3 Subˢ from Genˡ McDougall's Brigade ; 3 Captˢ & 3 Subˢ from Genˡ Varnum's, for Court Martial.

HEAD QUARTERS PEEKSKILL 27 JULY 1777

Brigadier Gen! McDougle
L! Colo [Giles] Russel *
Brigade Major Platt
Adj! [Elihu] Marvin

} officers of the Day.

A Piquit Consisting of 1 Cap! 2 Subs 4 Sargiants 4 Cor! & 50 Privates is ordered to Be kept at the Church below kings fery to take 3 Days Provision & to be Releavd once in 3 Days: from the Present uncartainty of the Enemys Distination they having Saild out of hook & undoubtedly Intend to Attack Some Place South *or* East of this & *that* a Conciderable Part of the Troops at Peekskill Will Be Calld to y! Place When Ever the attact Should be made the gen orders Persuant to y! Advice Rec! from Gen Washington that y! Several Brigades at this Place *be thoroughly* Aqu[ip]t and hold them Selves in Redyness to March at y! Shortest Notice

General Parsons & huntings [Huntington's] B D [Brigades] are ordered: Huntingtons to Peekskill: Parsons to his former ground on y! Left General Varnams Brigade is ordered to Incamp on the hill Back of the [   ] generals Nearer to general Huntingtons † genr! huntington's to Incamp *at Peeks Kill* on General Varnams former Ground: 2 Battallians of General Parsons Brigade to Incamp on the hill East of y! Generals *Head Quarters* Whare Colo Webbs (*Wyllys*) & Douglases was Incamed

---

HEAD QUARTERS, PEEKS KILL, 28 JULY, 1777.

Parole, *Albany.*   C. Sign, *Canaan.*

1 S 1 C 12 P from Gen! Huntington's Brigade to parade to-morrow morning at 6 o'clock with proper tools to clear & mend the Road from Peeks Kill to King's ferry.

1 S 1 C 12 P from Gen! Parsons Brigade to relieve the Cattle Guard at Crumpond to-morrow morning.

* Cumstock. *Platt.*
† "On the Hill in front of the Gen'ls near Mandevill's."—*Platt.*

HEAD QUARTERS, PEEKS KILL, 29 JULY, 1777.

Parole, *Glover.*   Countersign, *March.*

Gen! Huntington
Major [Hezekiah] Holdridge
B. Major [David] Humphreys   } Officers of the Day.
Adj! Selden

L! Col° [David] Dimon is ordered to march to fort Montgomery
to relieve the Militia whose time is out.

REGIMENTAL ORDERS CAMP AT PEEKSKILL JULY 29 1777

Capts & officers Commanding Companies to make out their Muster Roles Each Capt to make 5 and to Apply to the L! Colo for a
form : a Courtmarshel to Set to-morrow at 10 oclock to try all such
Prisoners as Shall Be Brought Before it Cap! [John] Mills to be
President all Parsons Concarnd to Attend y° Revalee to Beet for the
future Emediately after the firing of the Morning gun at Which
time Reg! is to Perade for y° Purpose of Exercising officers are Required to Attend : y° Sarj! Magor is Peromtoryly Ordered to Con-
fine all those Sarj!ˢ that are not Properly Attentive to their Duty and
if he Omits Complying with this order he May Rest Asured that he
will Be Sevearly Punished the Sarg!ˢ Must be Sencable that they are
Answerable for y° Least inattention the men Seem to Pay to their
Duty When in their Power to Remady it & May Expect to be punished According As the Sarg!ˢ are not Aproved of as yet By the Field
officers those that not thorough in performing their Duty will be
Reduced to do Privates Duty & those Cor! & Privates who the Commanding officer Shall think Desarving Shall be Prased for he is Determined to Reward them that behave Like good Soldiers and to
punish them Who by their un Soldier Like behaviour May Demand
it : the L! Colo is Surprised that After So many Repeeted orders to
y° Contrary the men Should Presume to burn Fences or Destroy y°
Property of any of the Inhabitence the officers are Calld upon : &
Injoind to Prevent any Such thing for the Future & to Indeavour to
find out those Who have Ben guilty that they May be brought to
tryal and Punished y° men in general are amaising Dilatory in turning out when Required the Adjtn and Sargt Magor are to Require

yͤ Sarjͭˢ to turn out their Men and have them on yͤ Parade Imediately when Required : those Sarjͭˢ Who Dont Bring on their Men
Accordingly are to be Punished but if yͤ men Refuse to Comply with
yͤ orders they Receive from their Non Com officers they are ordered
to Be Confined & they May Rest Asured they Shall be Punished
Sevearly :

As Commissioned officers of Companies Attend Role Call morning & Evening they will take Perticuler Care to Bring thoes men
who Do not attend and have no Leave of Absence to a Condine
Punishment

HEAD QUARTERS, JULY 30ᵀᴴ, 1777.

Parole, *President.*   Countersign, *Hancock.*

General Varnam
Major [David Fithian] Sill
B. Major [Ebenezer] Flagg   } officers of the Day.
Adgertent [Henry] Ten Eyck

Persuant to yͤ orders Recᵈ from Genrˡ Washington 2 Brigades
namely genrˡ McDougles & general Huntingtons are Emediately to
Pack up their heavy Bagage & Convey it over the River and hold
them Selves in Redyness to March with four Days Provision *ready
drawn to march* at a Minutes Warning and all the Partys Detachd
from Either of the Brigades on [*or*] any out Posts Exept the guard
at Danbury & those on Bourd yͤ Ships and Whale boats are *ordered*
Emediatly to Join their Respective Regiments.

The Garrison at Fort Constitution is reduced to a Capͭˢ command
consisting of one Company from Genˡ Varnum's Brigade. Major
[Ebenezer] Huntington is to return to the Regͭ & all the Troops
belonging to Genˡ McDougall's Brigade are immediately to join their
respective Regͭˢ.

Lt. Colͦ [David] Dimon is to march immediately to the White
Plaines with his Regͭ to relieve Colͦ Cortlandt & the Detachment
under his Command who are immediately to join their respective
Brigades instead of marching to Fort Montgomery, which is occasioned by the different orders since recᵈ from Genˡ Washington.

The Bridge is to furnish 9 Centries if Necessary. The Hospital guard four, two at each Barrack.

Mr. Simeon Belding late Q̲ M̲ of Col̲ [Samuel] Wyllys's Reg̲ is appointed Q̲ M̲ to Gen̲ Parson's Brigade.

HEAD QUARTERS, JULY 31, 1777.

Parole, *Jamaica*.   C. Sign, *Flushing*.

Brigadier general Parsons
Lt Colo [Samuel] Printice   } officers of the Day.*
Brigd Magor Humphris [David Humphreys]

John kenis (*Kavas*) of the 3 Pensylvania Reg̲ Commanded by Colo Ward (*Wood*) was tryd for Disartion the Court Sentance the Prisoners to Receave 100 Lashes on y̲ naked back Tomorrow mornig at Guard Mounting: Samuel oakley † of West Chaster County was Tryd for being an Enemy To his Cuntry & a Robber taking arms also as being Spy from the Enemy it was unnessary to Produce Any Evidence altho it Might have ben Produced y̲ Prisoner of his own accord Confes̲ as Much as y̲ Court Could Require to be Satisfied of his guilt y̲ Court Judged the Prisoner guilty of y̲ Crimes Eledged Against him Concidering the Extraodenary & Atrotious Nature of his Crime as a Robber & Spye from y̲ Enemy also taken in arms Sentance him to Suffer the Pains of Death Reuben Smith Tryd as an Enemi to his Contry & a Robber of y̲ well Effected Inhabitance the Cort agudg the Prisoner Guilty of y̲ whole Crime *and* in order that the Examplery Punishment May Sarv to Deter other Villins from Commiting y̲ Like Crimes Sentance him to Receive 100 Lashes on the Naked Body the first 20 of which are to be Inflicted on y̲ grand Perade the tomorrow morning

Remainder to Inflicted at the head of Each Brigade Day by Day Provided the Same No of 100 Lashes be not Deminished or Lessned after which S̲ Prisoner is to be Sent on Bourd one of the (*Continental*) Ships of war in y̲ North River there to Be kept to hard Labour at y̲ Same time to be Secured from Making his Escape During the Present war: John Hartstone (*Houston*) Cap̲ in

----

* Adjutant Hart.—*Platt.*   † *Lemuel Akerly.*

Colo gansaevils* Regt Tryd for ye following Charges first for Disurting to the Enemy While a Capt in ye Continental Service & after he had Rcd 500 Dollars Recruiting money and taking with him to ye Enemi Secondly for forfiting ye Confidence Placed in him by Colo Lamb for his going to ye Peekskill 3d for Disarting the gentlemen under *whose* Confidence he was Put in order to be Conducted to Genrl Putnam 4ly for Forging a Pass *signed* "by order of General McDougle Richard Platt Magor of [Br]" as to the first Charge of Disarting to ye Enemy ye Court is of Appinan that the Prisoner is *not* guilty *thereof. As to the Remainder of the Charges against him, the Court is of opinion that the Prisoner is guilty of the same* as allso Appears by his own Confession the Court therefore order & adgudg that ye Sd Hartstone (*Houston*) be Dismissed from ye army ye general approoves the Sentance & orders the BD [Brigade] Magor of the Day to see them Put into Execution as above Directed & that John hutson leave the Camp Emediatly Samuel Oakerly [Lemuel Akerly] to be Exercuted on Munday 11th Day of August next between ye hours of 9 & 11 oclock in ye fore noon ye Execution of Edmund Palmer & Amos Rose which was to be tomorrow is Respited till munday next at ye Same time of the Day ye Court martial of which Colo [John Durkee] Durkey was Presid[ent] President is Desolved

Brigade orders Colo [Samuel] Prentice Regiment to Furnish the generals guard tomorrow all the Musick in the Brigade to attend on the Grand Perade tomorrow morning Lt Colo Prentice Regt to

* This record well illustrates the difficulty of tracing the persons intended. "Gansaevil" is evidently intended for Gansevoort, and Peter Gansevoort was appointed Colonel of the Third Battalion of New York, 21 November, 1776. Hartstone or Hutson were not found in any New York Company; but Platt Orderly Book gave it as Captain John Houston of Gansevoort's Regiment. In 1775, Houston was a Second Lieutenant in the New York line, and when the force was re-organized at the end of 1776, was recommended for a Captaincy, as an "excellent officer and unprovided for." He received a commission, but the record suddenly becomes silent as to his service. I give in parallel columns the names of the three officers of Houston's regiments, the first column being taken from the *State Archives, The Revolution*, I, p. 140, and the second from *Calendar of Historical Manuscripts*, II, 49:—

John Houston, Capt.	John Houston, Capt.
John Welder, Lieut.	John Welch, Lieut.
Prentice Brower, 2d Lieut.	Prentice Bowen, 2d Lieut.

Send 1 Sarg! 1 Cor! & 12 Privates to Releave the guard at fourt Independance

Regimental Orders   Camp a Peekskill July 31 1778[1777].
the Court marshel of Which Cap! [John] mills was President is Desolved   No officer for the future will give Leave of Absence from Camp to any Soldier & None is to Be absent without Leave of one of y? Field officers & he is to have his Permition in writeing or he may Expect to be taken up and Punished   Captains or officers Commanding Comy s are fourthwith to Make out Returns to the L! Col? of the men they have in their Companies & Whare they are and those that Absent and by whose Permition &c y? L! Colo Recomends to y? Comisnd officers to turn out Every Day to inform them Selves into Every part of Exercise Nessary for an officer to understand y? Sarj!s & Cor!s are to turn out Every Day twice to Exersise By them Selves

HEAD QUARTERS AUGUST Y? 1 1777

general Varnam
Colo [Samuel] Wyllys   } officers of the Day
BD Magr Flag *
Adj! [Elisha] Hopkins

the Court of inquirery of which Colo [John] Chandler was President is Desolved the general has been informd that Much Damage has ben Done by the main guard in y? house whare it has ben kept By Cuting y? Pillars of the Peazza Pulling up the flore &c he therfore Strictly Injoins it upon y? Main Guard and all other Guards to take special Care not to Injure the Houses in which they are kept or the ajacent Buildings *under severe Penalties.*

HEAD QUARTERS PEEKS KILL 2 AUGUST 1777

Parole, *Cowardice.*   C. Sign, *Death.*

Brigadier Gen! Parsons
Lt. Col? Sherman   } Officers of the Day.
B. Major [David] Humphreys
Adjutant Holden

* Box—*Platt.*

Camp Peeks July   Camp Peekskills August 4 1777 Brig.ᵈ Genᵉˡ
Parsons Lᵗ Colᵒ Olny Brigade Majᵗ Omppres [David Humphreys]
Adjᵗ [Henry] Ten Eyck Officers of the Day   Genᵉˡ Putnams Guard
to Consist of 24 Privates the Genᵉˡ has Reason to know that the
attention of the Enemy is turned towards the North River and the
passes on the high Land Dayly and hourly Expects an Attack Recommends and enjoins it upon all Officers in this Department
Emediatly to Examin the state of the arms & amunition of their
men and See that they are Put in the Best Condition   the Surgeon
of Several Regᵗˢ are Directed to Make Dayly Returns of the Sick
under their Care to Doctr Burnet Surgeon & Phisition Genrˡ   Colo
[Charles] Webbs Regt to Furnish yᵉ generals guard tomorrow.

HEAD QUARTERS PEEKSKILL AUGUST Yᴱ 5ᵀᴴ 1777

Parole, *Barry.*   C. Sign, *Burk.*

General McDougle ⎫
Colo [Heman] Swift ⎪
BD Magor [Richard] Platt ⎬ officers of the Day.
Ajertent Royce [Nehemiah Rice] ⎭

a Fatigue Party To Consist of one Capᵗ 1 Sublt and 150 men to
Perade tomorrow morning at 6 cclock *to bring up the Boats from
Kings Ferry to Fort Montgomery.* A subalterns party of thirty men
to parade to-morrow morning at 6 o'clock with their arms & with
Six Days Provision from genrˡ. McDougles BD the officer of yᵉ Party
to wait on yᵉ general for orders yᵉ four Brigades in this Department
are to form 2 Divisions : Brigadier McDougle & Brigadier Genˡ.
Huntington to form one Intire Division Bd genˡ. Parsons & general
Varnams Brigades to make another Division to Be Commanded By
the Senier Brigadier of Each Division

The Detachment that lately returned from White Plains with
Colo Cortlandt have liberty to discharge their Pieces this Evening
at Retreat Beating under the Direction of their officers.

Brigade orders the Senior Field officer of General Parsons Brigade
to Command : Colo Wyllys to Command till Further orders in order
more Effectually to Prevent any Reledation of Disipline and Loss of
arms   one Company of Each Regᵗ in yᵉ Brigade is to [be] off Duty

Every Day & to Be Peraded with their arms & Accutrements and a Carefull Examination to be made at which time all yᵉ officers in the Camp are to be Present the Duty required of the Regᵗ are to be Done By the other Companyes and Defeerances are to be Carfully noticed the Companies Deficiancys & Names of yᵉ Soldiers to be Returned to yᵉ Commanding officer of yᵉ Regᵗ a Coppy theirof to be kept by the Commanding Officer of Companies Which is Carefully to be Examined with yᵉ Deficiances found and the next Examination for all which the Soldiers Will Be Charged and Stopages Made from his Wages unless they arise from unEvitable Providence or in yᵉ Way of his Duty a Report to Be made Every Eight Days By yᵉ Commanding officer of the Regᵗ to the Brigadier General as it is perticularly yᵉ Duty of the Sarjeants to See the orders of yᵉ officerr Carryed into Execution it is Recomended that they make Dayly Reports of the State of the Company to the officers & that Every officer make him Self thoroughly Aquainted With State of the Companys to which they Belong and at all times to Be able to Render a Particular Account thirof

Detales for Guard	Colo Charles Webbs Regiment					
	C	S	S	C	DF	Pᵗ
Colo Webb for Guard . . .	o	1	1	1		8
for Piquit						4
Fatigue for the boats . . .	1	o	o	o		8
for Common Fatigue . . .	o	o	o	o		2

Capt [David] Parsons * Company 1 Sarjt 4 men for Main Guard August yᵉ 6ᵗʰ 1777

HEAD QUARTERS AUGUST 6ᵀᴴ 1777

Brigadier General Huntington
Colo [Philip Burr] Bradley
Brᵈ Magor [Roger] Alden
Adjᵗ [Elihu] Marvin

} Officers of the Day

Colo Charles Webbs Regimen in general Parsons BD is to Be Mustered tomorrow morning at 8 [*fine*] oclock and the Comʸ of Light Dragoon † at Eight [*six*] oclock Do that the Workmen of the Ar-

* At this time a prisoner in the hands of the British.

† A part of Sheldon's Regiment.

moury Be Subject to the orders of Colo Allen the Superintendant.
the Commanding officers of the Respective Reg^ts are to give orders
for Repairing the Defective arms in their Respective Regts With A
Cartifycate how the arms Come Defective those that are Cartifyd
to Want Repairing by unEvitable Exident the armours are to Repair
without Chargeing to ye Reg^t. those that are Cartifyd to be So through
the Deficiancy of Soldier are to Be Chargd to the Reg^t An Account
of Cost and the Names of the Soldiers are to be monthly Transmited to the Comnding officer of the Reg^t Who is to Deliver the
Same To the Pay Master of Reg^t and he is to Stop Such Cost out
of the Defitiant (*defaulting*) Soldiers Wages

the Signal to be given by ye Sub^lin and his Party (*of thirty*) gone
towards Harvestraw & (*on*) their Discovering the Enemy fleet to be
Coming up the North River is a Large *fire &* Smoke on ye hill

BRIGADE ORDERS AUGUST Y^E 6TH 1777

all the Men belonging to Colo Demons Reg^t who have been Re-
leavd from Duty Sence the Reg^t Marchd or who have recovered from
Sickness So as to be able to do Duty are to joine the Reg^t at White
Planes without the least Delay   Lt Colo Reg^t * to Releave the guard
at fourt Independance with A Sarj^t Cor^l & 12 men   Colo [Samuel]
Wyllyses Reg^t to Releave ye guard at Robinsons Mills with the Like
Number Each Party to Carry 3 Days Provision   Colo Webbs
Detales for guard   S   C   D   F   P
                     1   1   1   1   8
       for Piquit   2

HEAD QUARTERS AUGUST 7TH 1777

Parole, *George.*   C. Sign, *Clinton.*

General McDougle †
Colo [John] Chandler
BD Magor Box   } Officers of the Day tomorrow.
Adj^t Leonard

Colo Angels and Colo Samuel B Webbs Regiments are to Be Mustered tomorrow Morning at 5 oclock   all ye Brigades are to Perade

---

* Varnum—*Platt.*   † Regnier?

to morrow morning on yᵉ hill By the gallows to Attend the Execution of Amos Rose & Edmund Palmor * at a genrᴵ Court Marshel held at fourt Muntgumery on yᵉ 5ᵗʰ of august 1777 By order of Genrᴵ Putnam Lt Colo Meggs [Return Jonathan Meigs] Presedent Samuel Gray a Soldier in Capt Hautrimacks Company Colo Douglases Regt Was Arained for Trval for Desartion found Guilty and ordered to Be led to yᵉ gallows with A Rope Round his Neck and their to Receive 100 Lashes on his Naked Back and Drumd out of garrison.† David Smith A Soldier in Capᴵ Goodens [Henry Godwin] Comʸ Colo Deboys [Dubois] Regᴵ Was tryed for Disartion and Sentanced to Receive 50 Lashes on his naked Back. Isaac Dolelson [Donaldson] A Soldier in Capᴵ [Thomas] Lees Company Colo Deboys [Dubois] Regt Was tryd for Sleeping on his Post found Guilty and to Receive 50 Lashes on his naked Back yᵉ General Approves of the Sentances of the Court Martial & orders yᵉ Prisoners to Receive their Punishment as Respectively ordered Excepting that Part only Respecting Samuel Grays being Drumd out of garison : that Instid of that he be Confined (*to service*) on bourd the Ship

at A genᴵ Court Marshel held at Peekskill August 5ᵗʰ 1777

By order of General Putnam Colo Samuel B Webb Tryd Lt Samuel Cringeon (*Simeon Cregier*) ‡ of Capt [Benjamin] Walkers § Company yᵉ 4 New york Battallion Was arained and tryed on a Charge

---

* It was in this case that Putnam wrote the curt letter to Clinton that is so often quoted as an example of his energy. Clinton had sent a flag to Verplanck's Point, demanding Edmund Palmer, then in the hands of the Americans, as a lieutenant in the British service. Putnam wrote in reply:

HEAD QUARTERS, 7 AUGUST, 1777.

Edmund Palmer, an officer in the enemy's service, was taken as a spy lurking within our lines; he has been tried as a spy, condemned as a spy, and shall be executed as a spy, and the flag is ordered to depart immediately.

ISRAEL PUTNAM.

P. S.—He has been accordingly executed.

A very fanciful account of this incident may be found in Bolton, *History of Westchester County*, I, 72.

† It was Samuel Gray, of Captain John F. Hamtranck's Company, of Colonel Lewis Dubois' Regiment.

‡ His name is not on the New York Revolutionary rolls.

§ He was later Aid to Baron Steuben, and in 1782 to General Washington.

brot Against him for Steeling from & Plunder the Inhabitents of
Many Valuable Articles when he Was Sent out with a Party With
Express orders to Protect them from being Plundered upon full
hearing the Evidence & the Prisoner the Court find him gudge (*and
adjudge*) him guilty of the Vialation of yͤ first Article 13 in Section
9ᵗʰ 16ᵗʰ Article Secͭ 13ᵗʰ and the 21 Arͭ Sect 14 of yͤ Martial Law
& there upon orders Sᵈ Ensign Gray (*Cregier*) to be Cashiered and
the name Place of Aboad Crime & Punishment of Sᵈ Ensn be Published in yͤ Publick New prints of yͤ State of New york and that
Sᵈ Cringeon (*Cregier*) Be Confined on bourd the Ships at fourt
Muntgumery till Restitution be made by him to yͤ Sufferers the
Genˡ Approves of yͤ Doeings of yͤ Court Martial Excepting his being
Confined on bourd the Ships and there upon Sentance Sᵈ Ensⁿ
Cregeon to be Confined (*cashiered*) and to (*be*) Sent under guard
to the Convention of this State to be by them Further Punished and
held till Restoration Be Made By him to Whome he has Plundered
as yͤ Convention Shall Judg Proper   the Commanding officer of the
Train of Artillery & Light Dragoon are ordered to Make Returns of
their Respective Companies at this and the ajacent Posts Emediately

---

DIVISION ORDERS, AUGUST 7, 1777.

One hundred and twenty men from Genˡ Huntington's Brigade
properly officered to parade at Gen'l McDougalls Encampment to-
morrow morning at six o'clock with one days provision without arms,
there to take orders from Colͦ Durkee.   Ensign Cole who has charge
of the Intrenching Forts will see them collected every Evening. He
will also at the same time return all axes to the Regͭˢ that are bor-
rowed of them.

The Service has been greatly injured by the Delay of making up
the Pay Rolls & Abstracts in due Season.   Genˡ McDougall therefore expressly orders that the Pay Rolls of each Regͭ for every Month
be punctually bro't to the respective Brigadiers the first day of every
Month after Pay becomes due, ready to be attested ; in Order that
they may be put into the Hands of the Pay Master, to enable him
to receive the Money for the Regiment, whenever the Military Chest
shall be in Cash.   Whoever fails to obey this Order, will be put in
Arrest.

HEAD QUARTERS AUGUST Yᵉ 8ᵀᴴ 1777

Parole, *Hanover.*   C. Sign, *Square.*

General Varnam
Lᵗ Colo [Josiah] Starr
Brigade Mʳ [David] Humphris   } officers of the Day
Adjᵗ Smith

Colo Bradleys Regt to Be Mustered tomorrow morning at 5 oclock are Directed to be Prepared Accordingly

And the unreasonable prices extorted from the soldier by the market People for want of a Rule or Standard to regulate the Prices of Articles sold in Camp shall be as follows : Butter, 2 / pʳ lb. Mutton & Lamb at 8*d*—Veal 6*d* Milk 6d pʳ Quart. Potatoes 6 / pʳ Bushel—Squashes 1 / pʳ Peck Beans or Peas in the Pod 1 / 6 pʳ peck. Cucumbers 1 / pʳ Dozen Pig for roasting 1 / pʳ lb. Turnips Carrits & Beets 6 / pʳ Bushel. The above Prices in New York Money & no Person or Persons in Camp may give or take for the above enumerated Articles more than the Stated Prices & so in proportion for greater or lesser Quantities on pain of forfeiting the Article or the value thereof.

The Provost Guard is reduced to 1 C 1 S 1 S 1 C 2 DF 34 P.

DIVISION ORDERS, 9 AUGUST, 1777.

One Hundred & twenty men properly officered from Gen'l Huntington's Brigade to parade to-morrow morning at six o'clock at Genl. McDougall's Encampment—there to take Orders from Colo. Durkee. .

HEAD QUARTERS, PEEKS KILL, 10 AUGUST, 1777.

Brigʳ Genˡ Varnum
Lᵗ Colᵒ [Giles] Russel
B. Major [Roger] Alden   } officers of the Day.
Adjutant [Thomas] Converse

At a Genˡ Court Martial held at Peeks Kill by Order of the Honᵇˡᵉ Major General Putnam on the 9ᵗʰ August, 1777, Samˡ B. Webb, President :

Cornelius Bradley of Cap! Humphrey's Company in Lt. Col?
Prentice's Reg! was tried for Desertion, carrying off his gun & inlisting again in Cap! Meads Comp⸗ —found guilty and ordered to
receive 100 Lashes on his naked back.

Thomas Spencer of Cap! Mansfield's Comp⸗ in L! Col? Prentice's
Reg! was tried for Desertion, found guilty and ordered to receive 50
Lashes on his naked back.

George Cook tried for sleeping on his post, found guilty & ordered
to receive 50 Lashes on his naked back, but as he had been unwell
for several Days & kept awake two or three Nights before, by his
Distemper, was then unfit for Duty & was standing up when found
asleep, — The Court recommend him to the Gen! for a Pardon.

The General approves the Proceedings & Judgment of the Court
Martial against the several Prisoners aforesaid & gives Sentence
against them respectively to receive their several Punishments ordered by the Court Martial to-morrow morning at 6 o'clock.

BRIGADE ORDERS AUGUST Y⸢E⸣ 8᠋TH 1777

Colo Wyllyses Regt to furnish y⸢e⸣ generals guard tomorrow the
Same fatigue tomorrow as usal

HEAD QUARTERS AUGUST 9᠋TH 1777

Parade, *Ulster.*   C. Sign, *Orange.*

Brigadier gen! Huntington   ⎫
Magor Hart [Hait]   ⎪
                             ⎬ officers of the Day
Brigd Magor [Richard] Platt ⎪
Adj! Marshel   ⎭

Colo Swifts & Colo Livingstones Regts to be Mustered tomorrow
morning at 5 oclock   the general is Surprised at the averices of the
Contry

Regimental orders Camp at Peekskill August y⸢e⸣ 11᠋th 1777

the Reg! officers and men to Be upon the Perade Emediatly after
y⸢e⸣ firing of the Morning Gun

A Very Perticuler attention to Be Paid to this order the arms to
Be Bright and Clean

HEAD QUARTERS AUGUST yᵉ 11ᵀᴴ 1777

General Huntington
Lᵗ Colo [Matthew] Mead   } officers of the Day
Brigad Magor Box
Adjt Hart

Amos Rose and Samuel Oakerly (*Akerly*) are Respited from Execution till Munday after Next a hogshead of flower was found buryd in the Ground in the Reer of Colo Wyllyses Incampment Any Parson Claiming the Same Will Appear and Make Evident their Property in Sᵈ Flour within four Days or it will be liable to Be used for the Publick

two barrels of good tobacco to be Sold (*at 7 o'clock*) tomorrow Morning at Vendue on the grand Perade Which Was taken from yᵉ Enemy

	C	S	S	C	DF	P
Colo Webbs Detals for Guard	0	0	1	1	2	11
For Piquit	0	1	1	1		4

Colo Wyllys Regᵗ to Furnish the generals Guard tomorrow Colo Webbs to Furnish yᵉ Guard at the Commisarys Colo Wyllys Regᵗ to furnish the Cattle guard this Evening

---

HEAD QUARTERS AUGUST 12ᵀᴴ 1777

General Varnam
Magor Johnson   } officers of the Day
Bᵗ Majᵗ [David] Humphries
Adjᵗ [Elisha] Hopkins

Colo Hughs D. Q. M General of this Department presents his Most Respectfull Complements to the Genrᴵ officers and Colos Commanding *or commanders of* Regts and others Who have had Clothing at the Qᵗ M General Store in Either or both of Preceading Campaigns and Begs Leave to Aquaint them the Accounts that Remain Unsettled are in his hands the Regimental & Brigade Q Mᵗ and Deputy Q Mᵗ genrᴵ of Divisions are forbid to take or Give any orders for forage without Permition from Capᵗ *Thomas* Campbell Forage Master for this Department at the Continental Villiage Colo Durkeys and Cortlands Regᵗ in Genrᴵ McDougles Brigade are to be

Mustered tomorrow Morning at 6 oclock and Colo Chandlers Reg.t with Cap.t Lees Com.y of Artillery are to be Mustered Next Day after tomorrow morning at 6 oclock 2 Subs 4 Sarj.ts 4 Cor.ls & 50 men Saylors if to be got to Perade tomorrow Morning Opposit to y.e generals in order to Man the Shark and Campden Galleys

Detales for guard &c

	S	C	DF	P
for the Galleys	1	1		11
for fatigue				2

Colo Prentice Regt to furnish the Generals guard tomorrow Colo Wyllys Reg.t to Releave the guard at the Comisary Store the Same fatigue tomorrow as today

———

	HEAD QUARTERS AUGUST y.E 13.TH 1777
Perole *Gates*	& Countersn *Troop.*

General Huntington
Maj.r Sedgwick
BD Magor [Richard] Platt
Adj.t [Henry] Ten Eyck

} officers of the Day

as the Enemys fleet have Disappeared for Some time with Evident Design to Supprise Some Part of this Continent and there is the Greatest Reason *to suspect* that they will Supprise this Post and that Very Soon. the general is greatly Pleased at the Sperit Discovered in the Millitia in turning out so Chearfully in Defance of their Rights & Privaledges Against our Cruel Enemy in this busy time of the year and that they *may* be able to Render the Best Service to their Country : the gen.l Directs the Commanding offiers of Reg.ts to Muster & Examin their Respective Reg.ts and Companies of Mellitia Respecting their Arms Accutrements and Aminition and See that they are Put in the best Condition and Report there Deficiencies Also that they Exercise there men from Six Oclock Untell ten in the Morning and four till seven In the After noon *every day.* Whereas the Gen.l is Enform.d that the Enhabitents Refuse to Sell their Milk to the Troops at the Staited price for Six pence per Quart which is a veary high price and Considering that it is of the Last Importance that the Troops be supplyed. and willing that the Enhabitents should be paid a Risonable Price for wh^t they supply the Trops with The Gen! Orders a brave and Prudent Officer with thirty men to be Detach^d from Each Brigade to Collect the Cows from these who Refuse to sell there Milk at the stated price in the Several Brigades s^d Officer is to take An Account of the Cows *their* No Marks Natural and Artificial. and the Owners names this to Be Done this After noon and S^d Cows to be Milked to Supply s^d Troops and kept under Guard till the Owners Engage to Sell the Milk what they Can Spare from there *own families* to the Troops at the Stated price the Gen Directs the general Directs the Commanding officers of Regts Emediately to Cause Every Soldier in their Regts that Shall be found taking or Robing Any Guardian of the Fruite or Burning Rails *or fence* Belonging to Private Property to be Whipt on the Naked Back at the Discretion of the Commanding officer According to the Demerit Not Exceading twenty Lashes without the formalty of Tryal By A Court Martial A Serj^t Cor! & 12 men is ordered to perade tomorrow morning at 6 oclock to guard A Number of prisoners to Sapours [Esopus] Colo Webbs Reg^t to furnish the generals Guard tomorrow & Cattle grd this Eveng

HEAD QUARTERS AUGUST 14TH 1777

Parole, *Danbury.*   C. Sign, *Litchfield.*

Brigadier gen! Ward
Lt Colo Wesenfield*
BD Mag^r [Roger] Alden
Adj^t Selden

} Officers of the Day

the general hereby Acquaints the officers of the Army that ye Barachs at No. 3 are thoroughly Clensed and to be Improoved as a general horspatal for the Reception of the sick and Wounded the officers and Regamental Surgeons in this Department are Directed Strictly to observe & follow ye Directions of Congress Respecting the Sick & Wounded Phisition & Surgeon gen! May know how to Dispose of them & Doct Burnet is Directed to Report Any that Shall Neglect or fail of this Necessary Part of their Duty to the Commander in Chief of this De Partment or the Director Gen! of

* Weissenfels.

this Department that they May Be Duely Punished : the Genr! orders
that all y? Drumers in this Department Make Returns of the State
of their Drums to the Commanding officers of Regts who is hearby
Directed to Cause those wanting *repairs* to be *immediately* Repared
& in future y? Drumers are to keep their own Drums in Repare at
their own Expence the Commanding officers of Regts & Companys
are to See that they Doe it and in Case of neglect the officers are to
See it Done and Stopages are to be made out of their Wages to Pay
the Same

The Regimental Returns of the sick to Doc! Burnet Physician &
Surgeon Gen! have of late been very deficient.

The Regimental Surgeons are enjoined punctually to observe &
perform their Duty in that Respect agreeable to the Resolutions of
Congress that the

1 S 2 S 2 C 30 P to parade to morrow Morning at 6 o'clock with
axes & spades to mend the Road from Kings Ferry to Peeks Kill.
The Party will receive the Tools at Q? M? Gen!? Store at Continental
Village.

HEAD QUARTERS AUGUST Y? 15.TH 1777

Parole, *Adams.*   C. Sign, *Wyllys.*

BD General Varnam
Colo Samuel B Webb *
Brigade Magor Box
Adj! Waterman
} officers of the Day

found By one of Colo Swifts Reg! in Last June A large Pack Containing A Regimental Coat faced with Brown with A Book & Sundry
Articels in it which the owner may have By Aplying to the Adj! of
S? Reg! and making Evident his Property   the Commanding officer
of y? Militia Regts and Companies are to take Spetial Care that
their *men* Dont go off without Being Regulerly Discharged and *that*
none to go without Returning *all* their Camp utentials flints Car-
treges & Every thing Drawn out of the Store on Pain of Paying for
those articles *themselves*   the Melitia in general Wards Brigade have
leave to Discharge their Pieces this Evening at Retreet beeting
under the Direction of their officers

* Colo Durkee, *Platt.*

HEAD QUARTERS AUGUST 16ᵀᴴ 1777

General Huntington
Magᵗ Holdrey [Hezekiah Holbridge] ⎫
BD Majᵗ [David] Humphris   ⎬ officers of the Day
Adjᵗ Royce [Nehemiah Rice]   ⎭

Colo Mosely Lost on yᵉ 14ᵗʰ Instent A Large Spyglass Shagreen
Case that might be taken Apart   Any Parson finding the Same and
will Return it to the owner or to head Qrs Shall Receive 3 Dollers
Reward and no Questions Asked

the Soldiers Who are Ingaged in yᵉ Eight Month Service Either
By Inlistment or otherwise Allso those of the 2 Battallion Raised by
the State of Connecticut untill the first of January [*June*] next as
well as those of the Melitia have Liberty to List into the 3 year
Sarvice or During the war Returning the Premiams they have alredy
Recd from that State in Part towards yᵉ Premeum to be Paid by that
State as (*to the*) Soldiers Inlisted in to the Continental Service as
Above Sᵈ : and those of the Eight Month men and of yᵉ 2 Battal-
ion[s] and those Inlisted as teemsters or Waggoners Must Return
the Premeams Recd from the State *of Connecticut.*   a general Cort-
marshel is Apointed to Set next Munday at 9 oclock at the Widow
Warrens Colo Durkey President

Lᵗ Colᵉ Wyllys, Majors Huntington & Stanley, 1 C, 2 S from Mc-
Dougalls, Parsons and Huntington's Brigades, members.

HEAD QUARTERS AUGUST 17ᵀᴴ 1777

Parole, *Tappan.*   C. Sign, *Bay.*

General Ward   ⎫
Lt Colo [Samuel] Prentice   ⎪
BrD Major Box *   ⎬ Officers of the Day
Adjt [Elihu] Marven   ⎭

* Platt.

HEAD QUARTERS AUGUST 18.TH 1777

Parole, *Burlington.*   C. Sign, *Slip.*

General Hunting[ton] ⎫
Colo [Israel] Angel   ⎪
BD Magor Box   ⎬ officers of the Day *
Adjt Rogers   ⎭

the general orders that all the Drum & Fife Magrs Make Returns Emediately of the Drums & Fifes in the Respective Regts also how many are wanting that they May be Furnished and Repared & after that the Drumers and Fifers are to keep them in Repair *at their own expence.*

HEAD QUARTERS AUGUST 19.TH 1777

Parole, *Putnam.*   C. Sign, *Webb.*

general Huntington   ⎫
Colo [Israel] Angel ⎪
BD Magor Box   ⎬ Officers of the Day
Adjt Rogers   ⎭

the general takes notice that the greatest Loads Drawn in Carts and Wagons are of hearty & well men Whereby the Teams are greatly Woryed he orders that no Soldier Ride in Carts or Wagons Except the Drivers and Sick Who are ordered to be Carryd on Pain of Being Whipt 20 Lashes on the naked Back   Such officers as have not Carryd in their Muster Roles to ye Deputy Muster Master Genrl. Will take Notice that unless he is furnished with Em by tomorrow morning 8 oclock they Can not be Included *in* the Abstracts *that* are Emediately to Be Sent to Hed-Qrts

PEEKSKILL AUGUST 20.TH 1777

Regimental orders Capts & officers Commanding Comys to Make a Return to ye Qr Mr of the number of men & of Tents and how Desposed of in their Respective Companies ye Qr Mr will make a Regimental Return of the Same kind & Deliver it to the Colo.

---

* Platt gives as the officers of the day : General Varnum, Colo Wyllys, Brigade Major Alden, and Adjutant Convers.

Prayers to be Attended at 6 oclock in y⁅ morning & Emediatly after Retreet beeting at Evening   officers as well as men will Punctually Attend

the men are ordered to Cook nowhare But in the Rear of the Reg⁅ at y⁅ Distance of 20 or 30 Rods from the Tents the fires on the Sides and front of the Incampment are to Be Put Emediatly   all the men off Duty Exipt those Imployd in Cooking to turn out to Clean the Perade & Streets of the Incampment   the officer of the Day in future to See that the Tents are Struck Every Day if the Weather will Admit of it and See that the ground is Properly Dryed

---

HEAD QU⁅⁅ AUGUST Y⁅ 20ᵀᴴ 1777

Parole, *Hempstead*.   C. Sign, *Plains*.

Colo [Charles] Webb
B⁅ D Maj⁅ [David] Humphris   } officers of the Day
Adj⁅ [Henry] Ten Eyck

at A gen⁅ Cort Marshel held at Peekskill August 19ᵗʰ 1777   Colo Durkey President Lt Roger More and Ensign David Russel [Resco] *of Cap⁅ Roger's company in Col⁅* [Roger] *Enos's regiment* Was Arained and Tryed for Mutiny & Disobaying orders and Refuseing to March and Secure [succour] this Post when ordered upon y⁅ 7ᵗʰ of this Instant Both found guilty of y⁅ Charge and ordered to be Cashiered the general Aproves of the Sentance & orders Lt Moure & Russel [Resco] to be Cashiered and to Deliver up their Commisions Emediately and Quit the Army   the Regimental Pay Master and [or] Commanding officers of Com⁅⁅ are Directed [*desired*] to Send Emediately to the Deputy Muster Master for their Muster Roles as he Expects to Leave this Post within a Day or two   the general orders that no officer or Soldier Presume to Ride any of the Wagon horses on any Pertence Whatever without A writen order from A general officer or y⁅ Deputy Quarter Master General of this Department   one Cap⁅ 2 Subs from general Parsons Brgd to be Returnd on genr⁅ Court marshel tomorrow morning at 9 oclock in the Room of those Who are gone on Comd

one Cap⁅ 2 Subs 2 Sarg⁅ 2 Cor⁅ & 30 men to be taken from general Parsons BrD to go to Fishkill tomorrow morning to Releave

Cap⋅ Catlin and his Party Imployd in making Cartriges & the men
Should Be Such as have ben used to Such Business   Colo Webb
one Subalton and Six Privates

HEAD QUARTERS AUGUST Y⋅ 21ˢᵀ 1777

Parole, *White Plains.*   C. Sign, *Rye.*

Colo Swift
BrD Magor [Richard] Platt   } Officers of the Day
Adj⋅ Royce [Rice]

if a Parson or Parsons of the Like [*following*] Description Should
Make their appearance y⋅ General orders that they be taken up and
Brought to Hed Q⋅ namely A lad About 17 years old 5 feet 3 Inches
high Slim built Pock marked has the Apearance of a Creeold Light
brown hair & Eyes &c   Colo Printice Regt to furnish the generals
gard tomorrow Colo Wyllyses Regt to furnish the Comisarys Guard
tomorrow

Regimental Orders   the officers Commanding Com⋅ are to Account to the Colo Emediatly of the arms Lost at the time When
Cap⋅ Parsons was taken

HEAD QUARTERS AUGUST Y⋅ 22 1777

Parole, *Baltimore.*   C. Sign, *Yates.*

Lt Colo Butler
BD Mager [Roger] Alden   } officers of the Day
Adj⋅ [Elihu] Marvin

at a general Court Marshel Wharof Colo Durkey was President
William Davis of Capt Barleys [Bardsley] Com⋅ Colo Swifts Regt
was Brought to Tryal for Steeling the 3ᵈ time the Prisoner Confesses
him Self guilty & Beggs the Court to have Compasion on him   the
Cort Sentance him to Receave 100 Lashes on the naked Back and
further order that he Be Sent on bourd one of the Continental
Guard Ships in the north River (*at Fort Montgomery*) their to Be
kept to hard labour During the war

John Benson of Cap⋅ Bettses Company Colo C Webb Regt was
Tryd for Disartion and Steeling Some good[s] the Prisoner pleeds

guilty as to Disarting & as to the Rest [*theft*] he Confesses he had
5 Black Silk Hankerchiefs and 6 Check Linen D.º that he gave 14
Dollars for and that the Same was taken from by one Heart by Virtue of an Advertisement   the Cort adjudges the prisoner Guilty of
the whole Charge and Sentance him to Receive 100 Lashes on the
Naked Back and then Sent on bourd one of the Guard Ships [*Continental Frigates*] and their kept to hard Labour During the Present
war   the genr.¹ Aproves of the Above Sentances and orders them to
Be Put in Execution tomorrow morning at Guard Mounting

GENERAL ORDERS HEAD Q.ᴿ AUGUST 23.ᴰ 1777

Parole, *Huntington.*   C. Sign, *Belfast.*

Colo Chandler
BD Maj.ᵗ Box   } officers of the Day
Adj.ᵗ Convearce

the general is very Sorry to See A Set of men in Camp Determined
to Destroy the Morals & Lives of the Troops as well as the order
and Disipline of yᵉ army by Selling Spiritous Liquers   he positively
forbids any Parson Selling any kind of Spiritous Liquors Exept the
State Comisarys to any Soldier without leave in writing from his
Commanding officer and in Case any (*Inn Keeper*) Setler or Re-
tailer Presume to transgress this order all his Liquers are Emediately to Be Seazed for the use of the hospatol   the general thinks
it Strange that there is Need of his Mentioning in order that it is
yᵉ Q.ᵗ Masters Duty to Receave take Care of and Deliver out aminition to the Troops as their is Ocation

John Chilson of Col.º Webb's Reg.ᵗ has lost a light brown Mare, 5
year old, 14 Hands high, trots & paces, main the off-side, short
tail, tapering &c., & offers a Reward of 3 Dollars & Necessary
Charges paid by him on Lieu.ᵗ Trowbridge of s.ᵈ Reg.ᵗ .

Strayed from the Stables at Head Quarters, a small chestnut col-
ored mare of the Naraganset Breed, full of Spirits, tho' very low in
flesh, small thin neck, with thick Bushy long main & Tail, trots &
paces, & gallops off—formerly owned by M.ʳ Bacon of Woodbury &
perhaps gone that way.   The Gen.¹ will give 3 Dollars reward to
have her bro't into him.

HEAD Q^{RS} AUGUST 24TH 1777

Parole, *Trumbull.*   C. Sign, *Wadsworth.*

Lt Colo Starr
BD Magor Humphris   } officers of the Day
Adjertent Ten Eyck

the General Court marshel Wharof Colo Durkey was President is Desolved a General Court marshel to Set at Fort mountgumery on Munday next at 8 oclock in the morning   Colo Deboice President the Prisonrs under the Sentance of Death now under the prevost guard have a further Restbit from their Execution untill the 2^d Munday of September *next.*

HEAD Q^R PEEKSKILL AUGUST 25 1777

Parole, *Willet.*   C. Sign, *Stark.*

Magor Heart [Hait]
BD Maj^r Platt   } Officers of the Day
Adj^t Rogers

Pursuent to orders Rec^d from general Washington the Train of Artillery at this Post and their Dependant are Directed to make Returns Weekly to general Putnam that he may Be able to make a general Return to General Washington of the Artillery at this Post upon the Present Prospect it is Probable the Troops will Remain hear Some time   the Commanding officer of Each Reg^t are Directed to Cause an aker of ground to be fixed for Turnups

the Seed the general has Sent after and will be hear Soon— *which Turnips will be for the use of the respective regiments.*

A Detáchment of 500 men Properly officered to Perade tomorrow morning by the main Guard *at five o'clock* under the Command of Colo Swift * and Lt Colo Mead and then and their to Receave their orders to have two Days Provisions Cooked &c   Regimental orders Peekskill August 25th 1777   those men that have not taken the oath of Fidelity to the States are to be Sworn tomorrow at 10 oclock officers Commanding Companies will make a list of the Men that have not taken the oath to Deliver to the Judg advocate Who is to Sware them

* Platt says *Webb.*

HEAD Q^R AUGUST Y^E 26TH 1777

Lt Colo Russell
BD Maj^r Alden   } officers of the Day &c
Adj^t Rogers *

Strayed from Genl Putnam's Stable a small brown Horse, about 14 hands high, Star in his forehead, snip Nose, trots & Canters well, has a Bunch on one hind leg just above the Hoof; any person finding him is to return him to Head Quarters & shall receive Six Dollars reward & all necessary Charges paid.

Thomas Sales [Yates] Esqr is Apointed Ad C to Magor Gen Putnam and is to be obayd and Respected acordingly the officer of the Prevost guard from time to time are to take Care that the Barrocks at No 2 are kept Clean

a number of Blanks for Regimental Returns are at head Q^{rs} Redy for the use of the Regiments

---

HEAD Q^{RS} AUG^T 27TH 1777

Parole, *Varnum.*   C. Sign, *Angel.*

Magor Johnson
BD Maj^r Box   } officers of the Day
Adjt Marvin

Lately strayed from Genl McDougall's Encampment a large dark sorrel Mare, well built, no brand, or Mark, trots well, has two Quirls in her forehead, is four years old—Whoever shall take up & return s^d Mare to David Lauret Junr in Col^o Chandler's Reg^t shall receive 5 Dollars Reward from said Lauret.

General McDougles † Brigade has Leave to Discharge their Pieces this Evening under the inspection of their officers

---

HEAD QUARTERS AUG^T 28TH 1777

Parole, *Plymouth.*   C. Sign, *Salem.*

Magor Sedgwick
BD Mago^r Humphris   } Officers of the Day
Adjt Waterman

* Platt says *Rice.*   † Platt says *Varnum's.*

To be sold to morrow morning at 8 o'clock at the House of Cap.
William Drake at public Vendue five Oxen, seven Cows & seven
Horses which were taken from the Enemy by Major Blagden's light
Dragoons, near Fort Independant on Fryday last.

Major Blagden's light Dragoons have liberty to fire their Pieces
this Evening at Retreat Beating under the Direction of their Officers.

HEAD QUARTERS AUG. 29TH 1777

Parole, *Davenport*.   C. Sign, *Eno*.

Colo Durkey
BD Magor Platt   } officers of the Day
Adj. Converce

a genl Court marshel is apointed to Set tomorow morn at 9 oclock
at the Widow Warrens Colo Angel President

2 Capts and 2 Subalterns from Gen. McDougalls Brigade.

1	"	2	"	"	Varnum's	"
1	"	2	"	"	Parson's	"
1	"	1	"	"	Huntington's	"

Gen. Varnams Brigade Excused from Duty tomorow for Brigade
Exercise & Scurmishes by firing Field peacs and Plattoons and
Each of the other Regiments will have the Same Indulgence in
their Turns

HEAD QUARTERS AUG. 30TH 1777

Parole, *Green*.   C. Sign, *Yates*.

L. Colo Levingston
BD Mag. Alden   } officers of the Day
Adj. Johnson

Colo C Webbs Reg. to furnish y. Gen. Guard tomorrow

HEAD QUARTERS AUG. 31ST 1777

Parole, *Norwalk*.   C. Sign, *Stratford*.

Magor Th[a]yer
BD Majr Box   } officers of the Day
Adj. Marshel *

* Rogers, *Platt*.

Major Ward is apointed a member of the Court marshel that is to Set tomorrow in the Room of one *of the Captains* in General Varnams [*McDougall's*] Brigade

Taken up a stray & bro't to Head Quarters: a brown or bay Horse, about 14 Hands high, four years old, a large Starr in his Forehead, white on his Nose, both hind Feet white, some white on his Forefeet above his hoofs, trots & canters.

Any Person that can evince his Title to him, may [have] him.

———

HEAD QUARTERS SEPTEMBER Y^E 1 1777

Parole, *Maryland.*   C. Sign, *Baltimore.*

Major Huntington }
BD Maj^r Humphris } officers of the Day
Ad^t Royce }

the Quarter masters of the Several Reg^{ts} are ordered to Carry in their Bill for Back Rations to the Comisary to the first of September Inclusively that they may be alowed & Settled According to their former Establishment

———

HEAD QUARTERS SEPTR 2 1777

Parole, *Franklin.*   C. Sign, *France.*

Lt Colo Printice }
BD Magor Platt } officers of the Day
Adjt Marvin }

the time for Mustering ye Troops in this Department is again arived the Commanding officers of Comys of artillery Light Draggoons foot & Artificers will Emediately Prepare their Muster Roles to the first of Sep^t agreeable to the Usal form & as the honourable Continental Congress Will Dispence with only three Roles for the future it is Expected that all 3 will Be acutely Drawn and Produced upon the Perade at the time of Mustering Compleetly finished no Excuse Will be taken for any Defetiances in the Roles Such officers as have not Recd their Muster Roles of the Last muster are

Directed to Send to the muster master at Colo Sam! B Webbs * for the Same

1 Cap! 2 Subs 3 Sarj!ˢ 3 Cor! & 50 Privates to Perade to Morrow with Tools Proper for mending the highway between kings fery and Peekskill the Duputy Q! Master will See them Properly furnished with Tools

Colo Webbs Reg! to furnish the gen! guard tomorw

HEAD QR!ˢ SEP! 3ᴰ 1777

Parole, *Philadelphia.*   C. Sign, *Chester.*

L! Col? Cumstock
B Major [Roger] Alden   } Officers of the Day.
Adjt [Henry] Ten Eyck

the Price of Cyder this year made in Camp Shall be 6ᵈ York morey or 4ᵈ Lawfull P! Quart and no more and Every Parson who Shall give or Receive more for Cyder than the Price aforesaid Shal' for the first offense forfit the Same given or Reᶜᵈ for Sᵈ Cyder ard for yᵉ Second offence Shall Be punished at the Descretion of a Court Martial

General McDougle Brigade is Excused from Duty tomorrow for Brigade Exercise Scurmishing and Firing Field Peaces and Plattoons those Soldiers that have Inlisted from the Melitia are Emediately to Join the army the Season Being advanced and the Days Shortned the time for Releaving guards in fut[ure] is to Be at 8 oclock in the Morning and *the Gen! orders that the Troops* Exercise from Revalle Beeting till 8 oclock and from 10 till 12 oclock & from 2 to 3 [5] oclock in yᵉ afternoon

at a general Court marshel held at fourt muntgumery by order of general Putnam on the 29 of August 1777 Colo Diboice President Capt Lee Garner [Capt. Lt. Gano] of Colo Lambs Reg! of Artillery was try[d] upon a Charge of Insulting [*assaulting*] Lt Colo Clory [McCloughry] by Confineing his Waiter *and* for taking [*making use of*] his own Property the Court upon Mild [*maturely*] Concideration of the Eviden[] Against Capt Lee garner Do Judg him not guilty of the Charge Cap! Thomas Betts an asistant Deputy Q!

* Platt says Colo Sam! Drike.

Master Genr! was tryd on a Charge of greatly [*grossly*] Abuseing
Cap! Gooding [Godwin] by [*of*] Neglecting his Duty and Expose-
ing his Property and the Property of the united States to the In-
clemency of the wet[her] and for Publickly Expressing him Self in
a maner unbecoming a man in his Place in the Continental Service
and a friend to Liberty the Court upon Marsh [*maturely*] Considering the Evidence Judg Capt Betts to be greatly guilty of grossly
Abuseing Capt Gooding of Neglecting his Duty and Expressing him
Self unbecoming an officer in the Continental Service and a friend
to the Cause of Liberty and that he Be therefore Discharged from
y.̣ army the general Aprov[s] the Preceading Judgments of the
Court marshel afores.̣ and orders Capt Thomas Betts Deputy Q.̣
Master Genr! to Quit the Continental army and that Capt Garner
Be Discharged from his Arest

Strayed from the Pasture of Cap! Wm. Drake a yoke of Oxen,
one a brindle bug Horned ox with a white tail—the other a black
ox with a large white Spot under his Throat about Midling size—the
Brindle ox the largest. Any Person who will return s.̣ Oxen or give
Information of them to s.̣ Capt. Wm. Drake shall be generously rewarded.

Stolen in the Evening of the 1st Instant out of the Holsters on
the Horse, a pair of very genteel Pistols, brass mounted, black Wal-
nut or Mahogany Stocks. A Hook in one to hang to the Belt more
than midling in Length, which pistols belonged to Col.̣ Eno. Any
Person that will return said Pistols to Col.̣ Eno or Head Quarters
shall receive 5 Dollars Reward & no Questions asked—& the Troops
in this Department on discovering the aforesaid Pistols are to seize
& send them [to] Head Quarters.

	HEADQ.ʀ.ˢ SEP.ᵀ.ʀ 4.ᵀ.ʜ 1777
Parole, *Wentham.*	C. Sign, *Mendam.*

Major Holdridg
B D Mag.ʳ Box   } officers of the Day
Adj! Waterman

No Parson is to take orders at Hedq.ʳ But Brigade Magors Adj.! s
and Comisiond officers. General Putnam Perceiving that *the orders*

of his Exelency Gen! Washington granting to Scouting Partys as a reward to there Extreordnery Fatigue & hard Ship & Dangers : the Plunder taken from the Enemy *to* Be Devided for their Benefit through unacquaintedness of those orders or some other Causes : has not Rightly Ben Attended to the Intention of those orders are not that any of the men (*our own*) or Enemys Stores Disarted (*discovered*) at any evacuated Post be considered the Property of those who first marched in, or that any public Hous discovered by Scouting Partys are to be Apropriated to them unless they find the Enemy in actual Persesian of them and Disposed (*dispossess*) them throff all Plunder taken under Such Surcomstances as by Sd orders is to Divided amongst the Corps (*captors*) ither by Contenen Troops or Melitia it is to be Disposed of (*reported*) by the Commanding officer of the Party to ye General *or* Commanding *officer* at sd Post Who is to Cause all Provision and Millitery Stores to be Aprised By the Comisary or Qr Master Gen! for use of the army and the Value thereof to be Paid to Sd Party and Such Articles as are not nesisary for the Use of the army are to be Sold at Publick Vendue under the Direction of the Quarter Master Gen! or his Deputy for the Benefit of the Captures (*captors*) Sd Plunder to be Advertised in general orders 3 Days Before the Sail & A Perticuler Description of the thing taken and Perscribed (*preserved*) by the Qr Master General or his Deputy that Any Parson Claiming Write to Sd Plunder may have oppertunity to Evince the Same.

HEAD QRTS SEPTR 5TH 1777

Parole, *Sweden.*   C. Sign, *Denmark.*

Lt Colo Shearman

B D Magor Humphris   } officers of the Day

Adjt Holding

Persuant to a Requestation of Governor Trumble the Command officers of the Respective Battallions Raised in the State of Connecticut to Serve in the Continental army Are ordered Emediately to Cause Compleet Returns to be made of their noncomisioned officers & Soldiers Inlisted or Detached to Serve in the 9 and half Battaln ordered to be Raised in that State Containing their Ranks & Names

& Names of the town in which they belong the time their Inlistment or Being Detached and the term of time for Which they are ingaged With a Perticuler account of those who have Disarted and [*or*] have *not* joined : also those who are hired for 3 years or During the War According to the Recomendation of Congress and by Whom they were hired to be Sent to Governer Trumble that the Cause of the Defetiancy of those Battallions may Be found out and Steps taken to fill them Up

the gen!. is Suprised to find the orders of yᵉ 16 of August Last Respecting the Melitia and 8 months men Inlisting into the Continental army for 3 years or During the war are Misstaken & Missaplyd the genr! had No Idea or intention that any in the Continental Service Should or Could Be *excused or* Released on Such Inlistments Nor that the Regulations of Congress Respecting two men hiring one to Be Ingaged in the Continental Service for 3 years or During the war Could be Extended to those who are allredy Ingagd in Service of (*for*) the war (*or*) for any shorter time to Excuse them till the Expiration of their service and all officers are hearby notifyd to take Care at their Peril Not to Prevart those Regulations of Congress and Perticuler States whare (*and*) the generals orders given out.

all Calculated for the Biseness (*benefit*) and advancement of the army to *the Detriment of the Army and the Diminution of* its uumbers by Excuseing Any who are Actually *engaged or* Inlisting others and all those soldiers Who have ben Excused and others Inlisting are ordered Emediately to Join their Respective Reg! and Both they and those and they that have *newly* Inlisted to Be holden till the Genr! See fit to order otherwise.

at a general Court marshel held at Peekskill By order of General Putnam Sept yᵉ 4ᵗʰ 1777 James Duggins [Duggan] of Colo Charles Webbs Regt was tryed for fireing his gun at a party of fatigue men as they was Coming from Work and uncaping another Cartradg to fire again are found Guilty of the Charge But are of Appinan that the Prisoner Ment to fire at one Barns Who had thretned to kill his wife the Court therfore Sentance the Prisoner to set upon the gallos half an hour with A halter Round his neck and then to receave 50 Lashes on his naked Back at the gallos the gener! aproves the Sentance and orders it to be Put in Execution tomorrow at 9 oclock at which time and Place General Parsons BD is ordered to attend

at a genr! Court marshel held at Peekskill Sep! 2 1777 Colo Angel
President Serg! *John* Dunbar Serg! W͟m Pack Park Sarj! Aaron Buck
Sarj! John Peterson Paterson Sarj! Newel Sabin [Noel Tabor] Sarg!
Josiah [Joseph] Brown & Francis Baptist W͟m Hardin Asa Luis
[Lewis] *Corpl.* John Goold Gideon Cary W͟m Lane W͟m Davis
Drumer[s] all of Colo Greens Reg! was tryd for Raising a mutiny
and on Tryal the Court is of apinan that the Prisoners are not guilty
of the Crime of Raiseing a muteny But that they are guilty of be-
having in a Disorderly maner   the Court therefore orders that the *six*
Sargts be Suspended During the Pleasure of the Colo[s] or Com-
manding officer[s] of the Regt͟ to which they belong   they further
order that the *others of the* above Prisoners be Repremanded *at the
Head of their Regiments by the Col͟ or* the Commanding officer of
the Reg! all Exept Cor! John Brown * and he is Aquited   Henery
Foresides † of Cap! Flaggs Company Colo Greens Regt Tryd for
Disarting his Reg! and Inlesting again into Colo Webbs Regt the
Court on Consideration of the Prisoners Crime and his Bad Con-
duct (*character*) Sentance him to Receave 100 Lashes on the naked
Back and then to Be Sent on bourd the Continental guard Ship of
war there to Be kept to hard Sarvice During the war   John Flitcher
(Fly) of Cap! Barnards Com͟y Colo Wyllys Regt was Tryed for Di-
sartion & found Guilty and Sentanced to Receave 100 Lashes on his
Naked back   the gen! Aprooves of the Proceadings and and Judgment of the Court marshel above s͟d and orders them to be Put in
Execution at 9 oclock tomorrow morning   W͟m Taylor Provost Master (*martial*) was tryd for Disobaying gen! orders in Riding the
Wagon horses belonging to the army   the Court is of Appinian that
the Prisoner is guilty of a breech of general orders But *not* know-
ingly & willingly (*wilfully*) Do Aquit him from *further* Punishment
the gen! aprovs of the Judgment and orders s͟d (*William*) Taylor to
Be Releasd from his Confinement

at a gen! Court marshel held a Peekskill Sep͟tr 5 1777 Colo Angel
Prsd Samuel Sturdavent ‡ was Tryd for Inlisting into Cap! Grangers
Com͟y Colo Charles Webbs Reg! after he had Inlisted in Colo Swifts

* Platt says it was John Gold who was acquitted.
† Forsy.
‡ Hardwant.

Reg! after he had Recd the Bounty the **Court being Convinced of**
his Villiany and that he Deserves an Examplery Punishment **Sen**-
tance him to Recv 100 Lashes on his Naked Back to be Inflicted on
three Differant Days and then to be sent on bord one of the Continental **Guard Ships there to** be kept to hard Labour During the
Present war the Gen! aproves of the Judgment By whiping him 34
Lashes tomorow morn at 9 oclock **33** next Morning & 33 on Munday morning the general Court martial whare of Colo Angel was
President is Desolved

HEAD QRTS SEP! 6ᵀᴴ 1777

Parole, *Christeen.*   C. Sign, *Elk.*

Colo Angel
BD M! Alden *   } officers of the Day
adjt Converce

the general observing some Inconvenianceys (*indiscretion*) in
granting Furloughs to the Determent of the army orders that for the
future No Furloughs Be granted to *any of* the Troops in this Department Exept by a general officer the Commanding officers of
the Respective Reg! are Directed to make Returns of all the De-
sarters from the British army in their Respective Reg! and Cause
them to apear tomorrow morning on the grand Perade

REGIMENTAL ORDERS PEEKSKILL SEP! 7ᵀᴴ 1777

the Regiment is to move tomorrow at 2 oclock on to the ground
Whare Colo Swifts Reg! formerly Incamped the orderly sarjts are
ordered to Perade the Sick Every morn before Doct Colmans tent
at the time he shall apoint

HEAD QRTS SEPT 7ᵀᴴ 1777

Parole, *President.*   C. Sign, *Hancock.*

Colo Charles Webb
BD Maj! Alden   } officers of the Day
adjt Johnson

* Platt says the Brigade Major was Platt.

the Deputy Paymaster Gen! has Rec! a form for General and Company Pay abstracts   he Directs the Regimental Paymasters to Call at his office for Copies   a Sarjt and 12 men are ordered as a guard over the Store at Peekskill to go on tomorrow morning the orders of yesterday Respecting those that Disarted from the British army are not fully understood   the general orders the Commanding officers of the Respective Regts to Cause their Capts to Examin their Companis and Report the number of British soldiers theirin and Cause them to apear on the Perade tomorrow morning at 8 oclock in order for their being Inlisted and Embodyed into one Regt agreeable to the orders of his Exclency general Washington that they may have an oppertunity to Distinguish them selves *pursuant to the noble spirit they have discovered by coming over to us.*

HEAD Q^{TRS} SEP^T 8TH 1777

Magor Ward
B D Maj^r Humphris $\Big\}$ officers of the Day.
Adj^t Rogers

HED Q^R SEP^T 9TH 1777

Parole, *McDougall.*   C. Sign, *Greene.*

Colo Swift
B D Maj^r Box $\Big\}$ officers of the Day.
Adj^t Rogers

The troops in the Several Brigades in this Department are ordered to Perade on the hill whare the gallous Stands at 9 o'clock to attend the Execution of Amos Rose and Samuel [Lemuel] Ackerley   the Troops in the Several Brigades are to Be Mustered Sucessively in there order viz general McDougles BD to morrow at 2 oclock afternoon General Parsons on Wednesday at 2 o'clock afternoon Gen! Huntingtons on Fryday 2 oclock afternoon   to Be Sold at Publick Vendue on Friday next on the grand Perade 21 Cows and one Calf and Six horses taken from ye Enemy by Colo Denmon [Dimond] the Vendue to begin at 10 oclock in morning

Division Orders.

As Gen! Huntington's Brigade is near Commissary Else, it will furnish him with four men every Day, if they should be wanted to assist him in the store and to cover the offal—and they will be allowed for those men in Detail of the Division.

Gen! Huntington will cause the Gen! Orders respecting the sutlers to be executed in the Neighborhood of his Camp—the Landing at Peekskill will require attention.

———————

HEAD Q̇ʀˢ SEPᵀ yᴱ 10ᵀᴴ 1777

Parole, *Bradley.*　　　　　　C. Sign, *Chandler.*

Colo Bradley　　　　　　⎫
BD Maj! Plat　　　　　　⎬ officer of the Day
Adj! Marven　　　　　　⎭

the Commanding officers of the Regts are to Cause Emediatly A Return to be made to the gen! of all those who have Disarted from the British Troops or Navy Since the Battle at Lexington and had never Ben in the Service of the united States Before they Disarted from the British army or navy who have Inlisted with Capt fallon from their Raspective Regtˢ in order that the Continental Bounty they have Red [received] may be Paid Back into the hands of William Bedlow Engⁿ Deputy Paymaster gen! in this Department Who is to Lodg his Receit with the Paymaster gen! * no Soldier who has Inlisted with Capt Fallon and has Cloths Suffitiant to Cover him til they get (*to*) Philadelphia without their Regimental Coats are to take their Coats with them those that have not are to take them the Sevear Season of the year is aproaching upon us and Many of the Troops ar Distitute & Stockens and other nesesary Cloathing which to suply one Commisiond officer of a Company is ordrd to go Emediatly home to Recrute and Procure those articles for their Companies and Return to Camp by the first of october next the Paymasters of the several Reg:ˢ are ordered to Pay those men who have Inlisted with Capt Fallon from their Respective Reg! to the time of their Inlisting with Capt Fallon or to give Proper Cartiycates for their wages Due and that Same has not been Paid Before they Marched from hear

* Platt says " with the Gen! "

HEAD QR.^{TS} SEPT.^R Y.^E 11.TH 1777

Parole, *Oronoko.*   C. Sign, *Firm.*

Colo [John] Chandler
BD Maj.^r [Roger] Alden   } officers of the Day
Adj.^t [Henry] Ten Eyck

HEAD QR.^{TS} SEPT.^R 12.TH 1777

Parole, *Liberty.*   C. Sign, *Property.*

Lt Colo [Josiah] Starr
Brd Magor Box   } officers of the Day
Adjt Waterman

the Reason of *some* Regiments being ordered to the northward *from the Brigades here* and *for* Some other Reasons A New Aragment is becom Nesery the Genrl orders therefore that the Regiments of Colo Durkeeys Chandlers and Bradleys form one Brigade and be Commanded by General McDougle and that the Regts of Colo Green Angel and Sherbourn form one Brigade and be Commanded by Colo [Genl] Varnam and that the Regiments of Col Charles Webb Wyllys & Samuel B Webb & Demmon [Dimond] form one Brigade and Be Commanded by BD General Parsons and that the Regts of Lt Colo Prentice & Colo Swift form one BD and be Commanded by BD Genr.^l Huntington

HEAD Q.^R 13 SEPT.^R 1777

Maj.^r Hait
BD.^{mr} Scott *   } officers of the Day
Adj.^t Selden

The Genl orders the following Resolutions of Congress to be publishd in orders, vizt :

IN CONGRESS, SEPT. 6.TH 1777

the Committee and Treasurer (*on the Treasury*) having taken into Consideration the Letter from General Gates of the 28.th of August as Neeting (*respecting*) Cloathing for the army under his Command aforded (*referred*) *to* them *by* the Congreass Reports that it appears from the Cloathier Genr.^l Report that he has ordered Considerable Suplys of Cloathing to be forwarded to the *army in the* Northern Department from *Boston* and he has Little Doubt of being

* Platt says Major Sedgwick and B. Major Platt.

able to in *the* Cource of 3 years (*the year*) to furnish the (*specific*) Articles of Cloathing Directed to be given as a Bounty to the Troops and as it will Be Equilly Disadvantagus to the Soldier as to the Searvice, Should they Receave the Money in Stead of Such Cloathing, the Bourd Disaproves of Stopages Made by the Deputy Paymaster General in the northern Department out of the Pay of the Troops in that Department on account of the Cloathing and Directs that the money Be Returned Exept in Case whare a Regt has Ben furnished with more Cloathing then their Bounty and that the greatest Care aught to Be taken to Doe Justice to the Soldiers as well as the Publick in this Asential Point it is the appinan of this Bourd it is not Suffitiant that *the* Clother Genr! Charge *the Regiment with* the articles Delivered and taken (*takes*) *the receipt* of the *Colo* or Commanding officer *and that the Colo or Commanding officer* on Delivering the Cloathing to the Captains or Comnding officers of Each Company takes his Rects Every Commanding officer of A Company aught moreover Strictly to be Required to keep A Cloathing Account with his Company Distinguishing the Several Articles Deld to Each Non Commisiond officer and Soldier and take Rects for the Same as his Vouchers and when Each Non Comsd officer & Solder Respectively Shall have Recd his Bounty of Cloathing ye Comisd (*commanding*) officer of the Company to whch he belongs Shall Deliver the Account to & Rects to the Commanding officer of the Regt to Enable him to settle the Cloathing Account with the Clothier Genr! as well as to Descover Whether Equil Justice has Ben Done to the Companies that Such Troops as have not Ben furnished with Clothing Aught to Be furnished with their Whole Bounty without Delay Which the Bourd have Earnestly Recommended to the Attention of the Cloather Genr! and he on his Part has Ingaged to Exeart Every means in his Power to Accomplish (*That*) Such of the Troops as have on their own Expence Provided any of those Articles of Cloathing alowed as a bounty or Shall Not have Drawn their Cloathing in the Cource of the year Shall be Intitled to Reccave the full Value thereof at the Everage Price which the Clothing Shall Cost the Publick & Whereas when the Bounty of Clothing was Provided by Congress it was Conceived that it Might be Impractable to obtain A Suffitiant Quantity *of cloath* for Regimental Coats for the Troops and for that Reason two hunting Shirts were Substituted but in the Event So Considerable a Suply has ben Provided that Clother Genr! has Ben Enabed to furnish more of the Troops with Regimental Coats and with hunting Shirts & Experience having Shewn that a further alteration of the articles of Cloathing as a Bounty may be made to the Advantage of the Soldiers & without Loss to the Publick therefore it is the apinan of the Committee that it Be Resolved that the Clothier genr! Be Directed to as far as he Shall have it in his Power to furnish all Non Comsd officers and Soldiers in the Service of the United States who have not Recd their Bounty of Cloathing at their Election Either with the Several Articles Allowed by Congress in the Resolution of the 8th of October 1777 (1776) or in Lue thereof the following articles Viz

 1 Regtl Coat at 8 Dollars & 60 Ninths [ninetieths]
 1 Jacket with (*out*) Sleaves at 2 Dollars & 60 Ninths

1 Pr Buckskin & 2 Pr of W or Linnen Breeches 8 Dollars

1 hat or Leathern Cap at 2 Dollars & 60 Do

2 Shirts	8 Do	
1 Pair overhalls	6 Do	First Cost
1 hunting Shirt	4 Do	Estimated at
2 Pair Stockens	4 Do	56 Dollars
2 Pair Shoes	6 Do	
1 Blanket at	6 Do	

But as the Cost of the Articles Last Specifyd exceeds that of the *cloathing allowed as a* Bounty for the troops *by* 8 Dollars and & 30 Ninetieths of a Dollar So much Shall be Stoped out of the Pay of Every Non Comsᵈ officer and Soldier who Shall Be Suplyed in the manner Last Directed as will make the amount of Cloathing they Shall Receave Equil to the Valley (*value*) of the Bounty of Clothing which Upon an Everidg of the Price of the Several articles is Estimated at 47 Dollars & 60 Nintiths of a Dollar the sᵈ Report Being twice Read on the Questian put Resolved that Congress Agree to the foregoing Report & Resolves By order of Congress Septʳ 6th **1777**

                                        JOHN HANCOCK Presᵈ *

HEAD Qᵀˢ SEPTᴿ 18ᵀᴴ 1777

all disarters and Prisoners are to be Sent to hed Qrˢ for Examination whenever Scouts are Sent out Notice is to be given, they are to be under the officer of the Day   the officer of the Day is to visit all guards & Piquits by Day and Night and make Returns Patroles are to be kept out & Sentinals advanced in the frunt of the Incampment & allso be under the Direction of the Day   the whole army is to keep 2 Days Provision by them Constantly and be Every way Equipt for Action   A Return of the State of the Respective Regᵗˢ to be made

WHITE PLANES HEAD Qᵀˢ SEPTᴿ 21 : 1777

officer of the Day tomorrow Colo Ludenton   the Same No to go on Piquit to night as Last Night & one   the Same roads great Care to be taken not to Put any on this Piquit But Such in whose Fidelity the greatest Confidence May Be Placed   Colo Ludington & Magor Gray will guard the Same Roads as Yesterday

Patroleing Partys are Constently to be kept up

A Detachment from the whole lines to Consist of 1 Colo 1 Lt

* With the entry of this day's orders the record of Platt ends, as he was ordered to the main army.

Colo 1 Magor 6 Cap! 18 Sub!ˢ 24 Ṣarj!ˢ 6 Musitioners and 100 Rank & File to Perade tomorrow morning at 9 oclock in the frunt of the Incampment With two Days Provision   officers of this Detachment Colo Charles Webb Lt Colo Butler Maj! Huntington

REGIMENTAL ORDERS

the Cap!ˢ of the Several Companies in this Battallian are forth-with to make returns of the Non Coms!ᵈ officers & Soldiers taken with Capt Parsons with their Names & the Names of those Disarted & the time when also the Names of those Decd and the time when Died   Porter Walbridge is Apointed Fife Maj! & is to be obayd accordingly

REGIMENTAL ORDERS 22 ᴺᴰ SEPTᴿ

the Reg! to Perade yˢ afternoon at 1 oClock at which time the arms & amunition is to be Examined   no officers or Solder is to be out of Camp on any account But to be redy to march on the Short-est notice the roasters to Perade with the Reg! at yᵉ above men-tiond time

WHITE PLANES SEPTᴿ : 22 HEAD Q!ˢ

the out Piquit to Consist of 50 men only   great Care is to be taken that the Troops are kept in Constant Rediness to march with 2 Days Provision which is to be Constantly on hand

the Paroles are to be Constently kept up as the Safty of the Camp much Depends on it   the guards & Piquits are to be kept up also Maj! Gray & Colo Ludington as has Ben kept Before

officer of the Day Lt Colo Shearman

HEAD Q!ᵀˢ yᵉ 23ᴿᴰ SEPTᴿ WHITE PLANS

the advanced Piquit to be the Same as yesterday till further orders frequent Complants having Ben made of Plundering the Inhabitent Robing gardings &c   the Genr! in the most Positive terms forbids any practice of this sort   we aught to Consider the Inhabitence al-ready too much Distressd & that we Come for their Protection & not for their Distruction   Small Scouts are to be kept out on Mild

Square & towards Stephen wards Patrooling towards y⁰ Enemy   to
Perade at 9 oclock in the morning 2 Sarj˖ᵗˢ & 18 men they are to
Return in the Evening & the Ranging Companies their amunition to
be Made tomorrow morning to the officer of the Day

HEAD QR˖ᵗˢ SEP˖ᵗᴿ 19˖ᵀᴴ 1777 WHITE PLANES
C S S C DF

A Detachment of 2 3 4 4 0 and 80 men Likewise 1 Field officer to Perade at four oclock and advance on toward Stephen Wards
& Mild Square and Patroole as Last night   Colo Ludington to furnish guards and patroles from the Camp to the North River Maj˖ᵗ
Gray to Send a guard and patrole on the road between Stephen
Wards and the North River on the Aproach of the Enemy 3 Canon
will Be fired in the frunt of the Incampment on which the Tents are
to be Struck and all the Bagage Loaded the Troops to be prepared
at their Several Posts as ordered

HEAD QᴿᵀˢAT WHITE PLANES SEP˖ᵗᴿ 20˖ᵀᴴ 1777

the Troops are all to Perade at their Incampments at 10 oClock
tomorrow morning all Reg˖ᵗ and Companies to apeare at their several alarm posts at Revalee beeting their Posts will Be asined them
by the Commanding officers of Reg˖ᵗˢ   Scouts are to be Carefull to
make Returns on their Return

C   Subs Sarjts

A Detachment of one Field officer   2   3   5   and 90 men
Rank & File from Colo Wyllyses Colo Webb & Colo Samuel B
Webbs Regiments are to Perade at 4 oclock this afternoon

officer of the Day Colo Wyllys the waggons & teems are to Perade
tomorrow with the Troops   a line of Cartrige to Be Placed a Round
the Incampment on Every Side and Every Person Attempting to
Enter is to be taken up and Examined   Lt Colo Butler to Command the Detachment

------

HED QᴿᵀˢAT WHITE PLANES SEPT 24˖ᵀᴴ 1777

Notwithstanding the orders of yesterday as well as Positive orders
Against plundering the Inhabitence Some Soldiers in direct opersi-

tion to orders and Contrary to Rules of humanity did plunder from
Mᵣ Burts a Calf the only Substance of the Distressd Family yᵉ
officers of Every Rank & and Soldiers are Calld upon in the Strict-
est Positive terms to Exrt themselves in Detacting the offenders that
Justice may be Done to the Ingered Inhabitents and the Camp
Clensed from the Imputation of Robery and Theft a Party of 105
men Properly officered to perade at 9 oclock with 2 Days Provision
Majᵣ Grosvener to Command the Party

Colo Butler
Adjᵗ Ten Eyck   } officers of the Day

Regimental orders the Colo is perfectly willing to Indulge Every
officer in the Regᵗ as Much as is Consistant with Duty & the good
of the service but he is perfectly sencable as Every officer of the
Least Consideration Must be that Every order General and Regimental must be Punctually attended to and Complyd with yᵗ order
is absolutely asential to be attended to in Camp and what alone
gives life and Sperit to an army & Could wish he Could be So happy
as to find that the officers by their Practice would make it Evident
that they are not Insenceable of it

he Cannot But Imagin that yᵉ officers by their Inatention in Di-
siplining their Comʸ and keeping up yᵗ order So nesary that they
Doe not Desire to attend or have no ambition of Exelling by their
Puntual attendence to Duty and is very Sory that he is under the
Disagreeable nesesity of Issuing orders to Compell yᵐ therefor the
Colo Recomends it to the officers to Examin the genrᵗ and Regimental orders yᵗ have Ben Issued & Espetially in Exerciseing y.
men Calling yᵣ Roles &c and faithfully Complying with Eᵐ the Colo
Expects that the officers Strictly Attend Role Calling & they are re-
quired to Punish all non Comsᵈ officers and Soldiers who Do not
attend to yᵣ Duty

Enos Fountain is apointed Dᵣ Majᵣ to Doe Drum Majᵣˢ Duty till
further orders & is to be obayd accordingly & is to take Perticuler
Care that the Several Beets beet in Camp are beet in their Proper
Season Sarjᵗ Lee in Capᵗ Hinckleys Comʸ for his missdemenier is
orderd to Doe Privates Duty

HEAD Q^RTS^ SEPT^R^ 25TH 1777

Maj^r^ Huntington   } officers of the Day
Adj^t^ Hunt

    the Genrl Directs that the utmost attention be Paid to Prevent
the Soldiers Strgling from y^r^ Regts that the Roles be Calld three
times a day at which time Some of the Coms^d^ officers will attend it
is Expected that all officers in their Several Ranks will be very attentive to the Disipline of thoee under y^r^ Command   Every Extre-
ordinary occurance must be Reported Emediately to the Commanding officer of the Corps in which it happens and by him to the
genr! A neglect of not Giving Intelligence of Disarters may be
attended with ye Most Disagreeable Consequences

HEAD QUARTERS SEPT^R^ 26TH 1777

    the genr! is happy to Inform ye officers & Soldiers of the Success
of our arms in the Northern Department on the 18th Instant Colo
Brown with his Reg! Attacted a Part of the Enemy at the Landing
Place Northward of Lake George and in a few minute from Whence
without Loss of time he Detachd A Party to the Mills between the
Landing and Tiantarague whare A great Number of the Enemy Was
Posted who were all made Prisoners a Block house near that Place
& Mount independence fell into our hands and were in Prosesion
of ye old French Lines and had Surrounded the fourt at Tye and
mount independence which by Later accounts are Surendered on
the 18th Capt Brown took 2 Capts 9 Sub^lts^ 2 Commisarys & 262
non Coms^d^ officers & Soldiers & 18 Artificers
    282 in the whole he took 105 Battoos in Lake Champlane & 50
above the falls Including 17 Gun Boats and one Armed Sloop 293
Arms and Retook more than 100 of our Prisoners
    on the 19th genr! Burguin with his whole force Attacted the Left
wing of Gen! Gates Army But were Bravely Repulsed

PEEKSKILL HEAD QR^TS^ OCT^R^ Y^E^ 1 1777

Colo [Samuel] Wyllys officer of the Day
    the Honourable Generable Asembely of the Stace of Connect-
icut having ben Pleased to Appoint Return gun Meggs Colo of the

Reg!. Latly Commanded by Colo David Dimon he is orderd to Join s^d Reg!. Emediatly & is to be obayd & respected accordingly officers Commanding Reg^ts and Cap^ts are Directed to See the teems anexed to their Several Comd^s are Imployd in Drawing wood for their Several Corps to Prevent the burning of fences the Melitia at the Barocks who have no Waggons will Aply to the Q^r master Gen!. for A Suffitiant Suply to Draw their wood

30 of the Melitia to Perade Every morning till further orders for fatigue they will Receave their orders from Cap!. Buckingham who will be on the Parade & Recv : them ye Black Smiths armourers & Carpenters Wheelrites & majours Who are well Acquanted with the Business are to Perade at Head Qr^ts tomorrow morning at 7 oclock

---

HEAD QR^TS PEEKSKILL OCTO^BR Y^E 2ND 1777

Colo Webb
Adj!. Barker } officers of the Day

A Court marshel to Set at Fort M^nt gumery to try Such Prisoners as Shall be Brot before it Colo Lamb President the members genr!. Clinton will Apoint the Commanding officers will make out y^r Returns of the field & Staff officers & of the Sarj!. & Drum & Fife Maj^rs & Qr^tr Master Sarj!. Agreeable to the form heartofore given by the Eldest Capt in making Such Roles the Roles are to be Cartified on the Back under the Proof of the Effectives By the Commanding officer of the Reg!. in the following Manner

I hearby Certify the above Role to be a true State of the Field and Staff officers & of the Sarg^ts Drum & Fife Maj!. & Quartermaster Sarj!.

Commanding officers of Companies will take Notice that no Return are to be made of the not Joind for the future unless they are well asured that such will Cartainly Join in a few Days and Even in that Case they not to be Reconed among the affective untill they Join their Respective Corps No Injury occurs to them therefor when they Join their Corps their time of Inlistment is to be mentioned and they will Draw Pay for the whole time genr!. Parsons BD has Leave to Discharge their Pieces at Retreet beeting

PEEKSKILL OCTO^{BR} 2ND 1777

Regimental orders Peekskill octo^{br} 1777 as the genr! has given Promition to the BD to Discharge their Peaces this Evening the Colo orders Every Non Coms^d officer & Soldier to attend on the Peɪade at the beeting of the Long Role one half an hour before the firing of the Evening gun*

HEAD QUARTERS OCT^{OR} 3RD 1777

Lt Colo Butler
Adj^t Hopkins } officers of the Day

Six men from the Melitia to Perade Every morning at the Comisarys Store they will Receave their orders from ye Comisary

FISHKILL HEAD Q^{TS} OCTOB^R 8TH 1777

the Continental Troops will Incamp on the ground near the Acadima the Melitia will ocupy the Barocks a Return to be made Emediately to Head Q^{ts} of the number and Deficiancy of the Troops in the Diferant Regts Both of the Continental & Melitia that they may be Compleetly Aquipt and fit for Action the Commanding officers of Reg^{ts} are ordered to See that their Several Corps Draw 4 Days Provision & have it Cooked Emediately and till further orders to have 3 Days Provision by them Redy Cooked that their May be no Complaint for want if they Should be Called to March

FISHKILL OCTOB^R Y^E 9TH 1777

the genr! is Surprised to hear that any of the Melitia who have Come into the army In Defence of their Contry Should be So Lost to all Sence of honour and of Regard to our Gen! Safety as to Abandon their Posts or to think of Disarting the army in this Critical Moment When it is Probable that the fate of amarica is Suspended on the Exertion of an hour or a Day he Calls on all officers & Soldiers of the Melitia to Exert them Selves as they Regard them Selves their Contry and the freedom of Millions yet unborn Prevent the Progress of the Army Northward which is undoubtedly Designd to Releave Genr! Burgoin & the officers are Directed to

Aprehend Every Parson found Desarting and Return them that they may be Punished agreeable to the Martial Law the Genr! orders that the Several Regts from BD: Genr! Wolcotts Brigade & Genr! Silemans Brigade to form one Brigade Including Colo hookers Regt Maj: Grav: 3 Cap!ˢ 9 Subs 10 Sarg!ˢ & 10 Cor!ˢ with Proper Musick & 300 Privates to form a Piquit at the lower barocks & to keep out Patrooling Partys

a Piquit of 1 Sub!ᵗ 2 Sarg!ˢ 2 Cor!ˢ & 30 Privates to keep out near the Ferry the genr!ˢ guard to Consist of; 1 Sub!ᵗ 2 Sarg!ˢ 2 Cor!ˢ & 20 Privates on the following Roads Viz one one the Rode Leading to Newfairfield : on on the Road to Danbury to take up any Parson Passing to or from Camp that have not Spetial Leave from a genr! officer one Serj: 1 Cor! & 12 men for Camp guard 1 Serj! 1 Cor! & 12 men for forredg guard the Troops are orderd to have 3 Days Provision Continually Cooked by them against any Suden Imargency   D   W

HED QR!ˢ OCTOB.ᴿ Yᴱ 12ᵀᴴ 1777

Lt Colo Shurman } officer of the Day

the genr! Imagins that too Much Cannot be Said to Rouse and annimate the Troops to a Sperit of behavior at this Critical Juncture takes this oppertunity to Remind that more than a Sentury & half ago our fore fathers fled from the Island of great Britan Crostd the atlentick to avoid the Cruel Persecution & oppresion of unrelenting British Tereny and Sought an assilleam a Place of Security then a habitation of wild Beasts and Savages Determined to bare the Fatigues & Dangers of their Interprises Magnimimity & fortetude in order to Procure their own Liberty and to Prepituate a [it] unhampord to us their Posterity for this they Left their Native Cuntry Pleasent Places & Rich Prosesions & with United hearts & Eforts Endured Hard Ships hunger and Cold Waiting & Coflicting with the Numerous Savages & for many years Lived in Continual wars that we Might Injoy the Sweets of freedom ; & by the Blessing Heaven they Conquered their Enemys & turnd the Wilderness into a fruitfull Field and from few in number becom a multitude (great) when the Invious Eye of Parsecution Herediteny to Tirents Grew Jellous of growing Posterity Race and Liberty of the United States of

America Began Many years ago to Prepare Chanes for America and to Presue us with Intolerable oppresion in their Exorbitant Demands upon us from time to time and now at Length have Drawn their Swords and Like outdatious Robers thretten to take away our Lives unless we will Surender our Libertys and Propertys which By the Laws of god & man we have the greatest Right to Injoy the activity & Motive is great Disolation & Destruction by fire & Sword makes the Progress of their Conquest

N B the Above orders are Not Half given out the general officers are Directed to give Discharges & Furloughs upon Applycation in Case of Sickness and for other Reasons as Shall appear Nesarry

HEAD QR.ᵗˢ FISHKILL OCTOBER 14.ᵀᴴ 1777

Colo Newbery
BD Maj.ʳ Humphris   } officers of the Day
Adj.ᵗ Waterbury

a Quantity of Cloathing for the Continental Troops in this Department are on the way hear and are Dayly Expected; Commanding officers of the Continental troops are to make Returns of the Cloathing they are Still in want of all the Troops at this Post Exept Genr.ˡ Sillimans Brigad are ordered to Perade tomorrow morning at 5 oclock at the Uper Barocks an 3 Days Provisions in order to March from hear; Genr.ˡ Sillemans BD to Perade at the Same time at the Lower barocks

OCTOBER Y.ᴱ 16.ᵀᴴ 1777 THREE MILDS ABOVE FISHKILL

Upon Receaving the agreeable News from the Northward that Genr.ˡ Burgeon and his army are all made Prisoners of war the genr.ˡ Congratulates the troops and orders them to Halt and Remain hear untill further orders and Cook Provision & Refresh them Selves and make them Selves as Comfortable as Posable holding them Selves in Rediness to march Imediately on further orders those that have no Provision are to Draw and Spetial Care is to be taken by the officers that no Injury Be Done to Private Property

FISHKILL OCTOBER 25ᵀᴴ 1777

Colo Webb }
BD Magor Chitington } officers of the Day
Adjt Hart }

the Commanding officers of Continental Troops or Regts are again ordered forthwith to make out A Return of the Cloathing Recᵈ and What is Still wanting in their Respective Regts the General forbids all Plundering of Private Property Robing Guardens burning Rails or fences under the Sevearest Penaltys the officers are to take Spetial Care to See that the Troops Strictly Comply with those orders and to take up any the See transgress this order

---

CAMPᵀ AT FISHKILL OCTOBER Yᴱ 26ᵀᴴ 1777

Regimental orders

a Regimental Court marshel to Set this Day at 10 oclk to try all Such Prisoners as Shall be brought before them all Parsons Concarnd to attend

CAPᵀ WALLBRIDG President

NORTH CASTLE NOVEMBᴿ Yᴱ 2ᴰ 1777

Regimental orders it is a genrl Complaint among the Inhabitence a Complaint two Justly founded that the Troops whare Ever Incamped Burn their fences and Destroy ther Property by Robing their Fields gardens &c a Practice that Every officer in Deed is Spetially Bound to Prevent the Lt Colo therefore orders in the Most Preamtory terms that no Soldier in future Be guilty of any of those Crimes on the Penalty of being Punished with the greatest Severity

Any Soldier found Pulling Down fences Burning Rails Robing of Feilds or gardins of the Inhabitence will be Whipt as many Lashes as the Commanding officer Shall think for he has Determined on a march Never to Call a Court Marshel to try offenders But to Punish them as he Shall think most Conveniant to good order and the good of the Service and the man found Standing by a fire made of Rails will be Deamed Equilly Guilty with him that Stole them and will be Punished accordingly the Lt Colo Expects that these orders will be Red to the Companis and that they will Punctually Comply with the Same which they will Doe if they have any Regard to their own Cost and Reputation

they Need not Expect to have Similar orders Every time we Tramp for those are allways to be obayd whether in Camp or on a March the men for the future will take Care not to Quit the Ranks when on the march or to be without hearing of the Drum if they Doe the Marshel Law in its greatest Vigor will be Put in Execution the Regt to march tomorrow morning at 7 oclock Every thing to be in Redeness

CAMP AT KING STREET NOV.ᴿ Yᴱ 4ᵀᴴ 1777
Regimental orders

as it is Leasure of time the Capᵗˢ and Commding officers of Companies will give orders to their men to wash and Clense their Arms that they may appear in a Soldier like maner when on the Perade a Return to be made to the Lt Colo Similar, to the Weekly Return by 12 oclock   a Return to Be made of the Clothing Still wanting that their may be no Delay of Drawing when the Cloths Come

REGIMENTAL ORDERS NOVᴹᴿ 13ᵀᴴ 1777

A Court Martial to Set this Day at 9 oclock to Try all Such Prisoners as Shall Be Brought Before them   at a genrl Court Martial held at Adjt Ten Eycks Markey By order of Colo Webb octobʳ 27ᵗʰ 1777 Continued by Several agurnments to Novᵐʳ 6ᵗʰ 1777 at Capt Wallbridges Qᴿ Capt Wallbridge President Lt Shipman Lt Chepman Lt Eldridge & Lt Benham membrs *

* The next entry in this Orderly Book was made after the regiment had joined the main army under Washington.

www.ingramcontent.com/pod-product-compliance
Lightning Source LLC
Chambersburg PA
CBHW021420090426
42742CB00009B/1193